Laughter and the Grace of God

Laughter and the Grace of God

Restoring Laughter to its Central Role
in Christian Faith and Theology

Brian Edgar

The Lutterworth Press

The Lutterworth Press
P.O. Box 60
Cambridge
CB1 2NT
United Kingdom

www.lutterworth.com
publishing@lutterworth.com

Paperback ISBN: 978 0 7188 9555 6
PDF ISBN: 978 0 7188 48149

British Library Cataloguing in Publication Data
A record is available from the British Library

First published by The Lutterworth Press, 2020
Copyright © Brian Edgar, 2019

Published by arrangement
with Cascade Books

All rights reserved. No part of this edition may be reproduced, stored electronically or in any retrieval system, or transmitted in any form or by any means, electronic, mechanical, photocopying, recording, or otherwise, without prior written permission from the Publisher (permissions@lutterworth.com).

*To Georgia, Blade, Jasmine and Lizzie.
May they laugh with God.*

*Laughter may be the only way to engage seriously
with the living God.*

—Charles L. Campbell

Contents

Preface | ix

1. Humor and the Christian Vision | 1
2. Mapping the Theo-Comical Territory | 7
3. Jesus the Laugh-Maker | 22
4. Parables, Comic Characters, and the Gospel | 33
5. Laughter as the Language of Faith | 48
6. Covenant Laughter and the Comic Vision | 57
7. God, Heaven, and Humor | 69
8. Grace and Truth through Laughter | 89
9. Laughter at the Cross | 103
10. The Comic Christian Life | 123

Bibliography | 137
Subject Index | 145
Name Index | 149
Scripture Index | 152

Preface

Only a fool raises his voice in laughter.
—Sirach 21:20

Writing about laughter is about as enjoyable a project as one can have, not only because one keeps coming across the genuinely funny, but also because as the subject develops it becomes increasingly clear that humor is not a trivial or merely light-hearted part of life but rather an aspect of human being that is fundamentally important in learning to love, developing community, and, especially, in forming a relationship with God. Laughter lies at the heart of Christian spirituality and theology.

The notion that laughter is so important has not, it must be conceded, been all that common. Many parts of the Christian tradition, both ancient and modern, have not only had less positive things to say about laughter, they have actively seen laughter as contrary to any kind of spiritual development. The ancient but influential *Rule Of Benedict*, for example, sets out twelve essential steps to take towards that humility which is necessary to attain "that perfect love which casts out fear" (1 John 4:18). If the *Rule* is right then the tenth step definitely rules out my own quest for perfect love on the basis that this is only achievable by one who "is not given to ready laughter, for it is written: Only a fool raises his voice in laughter (Sirach 21:23)." What this might mean for someone who goes even further and writes positively about the spiritual significance of laughter I am not sure. Anyway, in case one misses the significance of the tenth step for some reason, perhaps hoping that there was some kind of mistake, the eleventh step is simply a reminder and reaffirmation of the tenth step, saying that maturity is gained by one who "speaks gently and without laughter." On this basis the twelfth and final step to humility remains unattainable and perfect love an impossibility. In more contemporary times humor has been significantly rehabilitated and seen as an important and valuable part of life that promotes health and enhances relationships. Yet the spiritual significance of laughter remains under question with its apparent triviality challenging the seriousness of discipleship. In *Laughter and the Grace of God* I take the contrary view and argue that the theological role of humor has been underestimated, that laughter is no impediment to holiness and that a sense of humor is an essential part of our relationship with God. For God has a good sense of humor as well. And laughter is an excellent way to both show love and cast out fear. Laughing at evil and the devil in all its forms is a good and biblical way of overcoming its power. Moreover, as it will be shown, laughter is not only not opposed to achieving love, it is in fact not possible to genuinely love another without laughter. And the great Christian themes of incarnation, crucifixion, resurrection, and sanctification cannot be either understood or lived without laughter. The tragedy is that the church has for so long so neglected, and has even feared and repudiated, this great gift of God. This book aims to restore laughter to its proper place in relationships with God, in the life of the church, and in theological reflection.

Laughter and the Grace of God is the continuation, and the conclusion, of a loose series of four books that began with an exploration of trinitarian theology in *The Message of the Trinity: Life in God* (InterVarsity 2004) and especially the notion that this doctrine is a way of expressing the truth that the believer actually shares in the life of God. This strongly participatory understanding of the Trinity led on to reflections on the nature of the relationship that develops, and *God is Friendship: A Theology of Spirituality, Community and Society* (Seedbed 2013) explores the intimacy of relationship with the gracious God who does not want servants so much as friends. The implications of this for understanding the importance of a playful attitude towards God and in the spiritual life generally were not immediately apparent to me and it required some fairly direct (and playful) intervention by God to get me to focus upon it in *The God Who Plays: A Playful Approach to Theology and Spirituality* (Cascade 2017). The central role laughter plays, and the sad theological neglect of the concept in the life of the church, became apparent during the writing of that book and so a fourth and final volume (unless God has another joke in store) has emerged. *Laughter and the Grace of God* puts laughter at the heart of our relationship with God and laughter's importance is far greater than the proportion of time that it might occupy in a relationship. The book considers the role that laughter plays in Scripture, in the life and ministry of Jesus, in Christian discipleship, and in the structure of theology.

Once again I am grateful to Asbury Theological Seminary, the President, Dr. Timothy Tennent, my colleagues on the faculty, and the Board of Trustees for the semester sabbatical that enabled me to do much of the writing. It is a privilege to have time set apart for thought, study, and writing. I am even more grateful to my wife, Barbara, who, as always, has provided great love and support. I think we have laughed more than ever of late.

May God bless with the gift of joy and laughter all who read this book.

1

Humor and the Christian Vision

Life is serious all the time, but living cannot be.
You may have all the solemnity you wish in your neckties,
but in anything important (such as sex, death, and religion),
you must have mirth or you will have madness.

—G. K. Chesterton[1]

It was another work day and Sue rose early and smiled at the sight of Michael's somewhat odd and contorted expression as he slept. And so she made a mental note to keep that in mind as a potential joke about his "beautiful" expression later in the day. While reading the newspaper she grinned somewhat wryly at a political opinion piece that made fun of a well-known politician's propensity for changing his mind. Then, of course, she checked out the cartoons. There was lots of laughter on the radio while Sue was traveling in the car and there were a few jokes with colleagues before they really got to work. Without really thinking too much about it she made a somewhat self-deprecating comment in an email that hopefully would ease the disappointment of her negative response to the request that had been made. Over the course of that day, and of all her other days, she experienced the humor of life: jokes, puns, quips, gags and tall stories, irony, wit, slapstick, farce, satire, tomfoolery, banter, sarcasm, leg-pulling, mockery, lampooning, parody, facetiousness, absurdity, teasing, caricaturing, eccentricity, paradox, clowning, whimsy, drollery, and tickling. Without her realizing it humor pervaded her life. There was humor of one kind or another in her friendships, her work, her church, and her prayer

1. Chesterton, *Lunacy and Letters*, 97.

life. Well actually, to tell the truth, three out of four is not too bad. (You can decide which was the odd one out.) These could produce various responses: a belly laugh, simple laughter, chuckles, giggles, smiles, grins, wry smiles, raised eyebrows, or simply an unperceivable, internal recognition of some whimsical incongruity, paradox, or parody.

The reality is that humor is everywhere, and the jokes and quips, the teasing and the clowning and the laughter and smiles in response to them represent only the external aspects of it. Humor is an essential part of human relationships and an expression of our nature. Humor emerges from an internal sense that is an aspect of temperament. Our "sense of humor" is part of who we are and, to a significant extent, the reality is that *we create humor when we perceive it*. Even when it is based on some external situation it is not really the situation that is comic (although we might describe it that way). No incongruity or situation is funny unless *we think* it is. It is *the sense* of humor that is critical and so the underlying temperament is far more important. It is necessary to describe humor as involving jokes, wit, cartoons, drollery, and so forth, but they alone are simply not an adequate summary or representation of the nature of humor. Humor is a temperament, a particular approach to life.

But what has this to do with theology and the spiritual life? This is a book about the biblical, theological, and spiritual importance of laughter and humor of various kinds. *I will suggest that despite (and to some extent because of) our culture's widespread use of humor that it has actually been theologically neglected and spiritually misunderstood.*

In developing this it will be shown that humor is largely about recognizing incongruity. This will be an important theme. Incongruity is found in virtually every joke, as in this one: "When I was a child I used to pray every night for a new bike, but then I realized the Lord doesn't work that way. So I stole one and asked him to forgive me instead." Perhaps one ought not make too much out of a single, simple joke, but I will make two points. Firstly, the depth of insight involved in understanding the joke is important. Being able to comprehend it means more than understanding about stealing bikes, it requires understanding about law, grace, forgiveness, and human frailty. Anyone who does not understand the humor in that situation will also never recognize false piety in church, insincerity in politics, or hypocrisy in anyone. A sense of humor that perceives incongruity is essential for understanding life. Only then can one see the incongruities of wealth and poverty and the implications that emerge from it (to which some people are amazingly blind) or the incongruity of the powerful and the weak, and of injustices of various kinds. As one explores the significance of a sense of humor one understands not only humor but the serious dimension of life much more fully. But that is only half of it.

The second point concerns the response to the joke which in this case is usually some form of (perhaps muted) laughter. What does that imply? The one who has what Conrad Heyers calls a "comic vision" of life may well respond to some of life's incongruities and injustices by weeping rather than by laughing, but overall they will be a person who laughs, who has confidence in God, who is certain that the last laugh belongs to God and that in the end all will be put right.[2]

In this book I will be presenting a theologically strong view of humor and laughter. That is, where humor is seen as being closely related to central theological themes, and as having extensive implications throughout life and faith. This view is strong in comparison to most other theologies of laughter where laughter and humor are variously ignored, viewed as morally suspect, or limited in scope. There are some who appreciate the value of humor as a characteristic of human life but who do not explore the implications for the spiritual dimension of life. There are some who see the importance of humor as an integral part of the mature spiritual life, but I will be making the stronger claim *that humor is part of relationship with God, an aspect of divine character, closely related to the central theological themes of incarnation, cross, and resurrection, and that it is an element of the Apostle Peter's declaration that "you may participate in the divine nature"* (2 Pet 1:4).

A theology of laughter

Humor is, I argue, an essential part of the Christian vision, part of the meaning and purpose of life. I will make a serious argument for joy, humor, and laughter as part of a healthy spiritual life. As that great advocate of religious humor, G. K. Chesterton, said, "Life is serious all the time, but living cannot be. You may have all the solemnity you wish in your neckties, but in anything important (such as sex, death, and religion), you must have mirth or you will have madness."[3] Humor, and its close relative, joy, is intrinsic to the nature of the gospel. Laughter has a redemptive dimension. It is part of the playful nature of relationships that is central to a relationship with God. This

---

2. Hyers, *The Comic Vision*.
3. Chesterton, *Lunacy and Letters*, 97.

argument about humor and laughter follows on from *The God Who Plays*, in which I argue that play is the essential and ultimate form of relationship with God. A playful attitude, I suggest, lies at the very heart of all spirituality and is critical for the whole of life. It is inevitable that some people will have difficulty in taking such a proposal seriously. But perhaps that is appropriate, not because play is trivial but because, as the great theorist of play Johan Huizinga argued, play is of a higher order than seriousness. Only a playful way of living, he suggested, does justice to the seriousness of life,[4] and as we shall see, humor is an important aspect of play.

Although humor can be misused in order to hurt and offend people, in its usual form it should be seen as a virtue, a disposition that is fundamentally good. It is an essential part of relationships between believers in the life of the church and socially important for the good order of society. But humor is not only of value in the present age, it is a present image of the future life of the eschatological kingdom of God. It is an earthly anticipation of divine joy, an example of life in the kingdom. As such it is for us now a means to self-knowledge and understanding, and a means of discerning truth, rationality, order, structure, and promoting wisdom.

Humor is, as we shall see, closely related to joy, hope, and faith. It is a part of the nature of God and an element of human participation with the divine. It is part of the kind of relationship that God wants with us. It is also, it must be said, something of a mystery, a hard-to-fully-define aspect of human and divine nature. It is revelatory in that an understanding of humor illuminates our understanding of the nature of both humanity and divinity. In reflecting on humor one also learns about the other parts of life as well. One cannot understand humor without understanding non-humor. In this way one creates a theology of laughter. "A theology of laughter deserves the name only if it can understand the reality of God himself in the light of the category of laughter and define the function of such talk of God for men and women and their existence in the world."[5]

This is, in fact both "a theology of laughter" *and* "a laughter theology" (or perhaps "a comic theology"). On the one hand, a theology of laughter is a theological exploration of humor and laughter in all its forms. It examines the theological, ethical, and spiritual implications of humor and comedic thinking. On the other hand, a comic theology is one where the notion of comic thinking and laughter influences the form and structure of

---

4. Huizinga, *Homo Ludens*, 211–12.
5. Kuschel, *Laughter*, xviii.

theology itself. It is not merely a theological examination of one aspect of God's world, it is a theology that recognizes the critical place that humor plays and allows it to influence the understanding of the whole structure of theology. This is that. Perhaps this is what Chesterton was implying when he said that the religion of the future will be based on a highly developed and subtle form of humor.[6]

Having said what this study is about, let me emphasis what humor, and this study of it, *are not*. Humor is not morally wrong, it is not even ambiguous in nature, but rather it is a moral good. It is not merely incidental to life, but is part of relationships of all kinds. Consequently, it is not theologically peripheral but central. It is not a phenomenon that is restricted to the present age, it is part of the life of the kingdom. It is not merely a human good but an essential part of relationship with God. It is not contrary to the centrality or seriousness of the cross of Christ, nor to suffering. It is complementary to them and revelatory in terms of the nature of God. Consequently, it should be clear that this focus on humor is not simply an accommodation to the entertaining, consumeristic spirit of the times. Indeed, the concept of humor presented here is not limited to lightweight contemporary, individualistic notions—it incorporates the classic sense of humor that sees scorn, mockery, and derision not as aberrations of humor but as part of it. I especially note that this is not just a book about jokes. The most significant dimension of laughter for our purposes lies in the disposition, the attitude, the temperament that determines one's mode of life. Indeed, I did consider that the funniest way to deal with the expectation that this was about jokes might be to write a book about humor that did not contain a single joke. But that proved impractical (and less interesting). This is not only not "a joke book," it is not "a history" of jokes or of humor. Although historical material is included this is not a history of humor and the various analyses and observations concerning historical situations and theories are simply included to illuminate the present argument about the central nature of humor and laughter in Christian faith and theology.

Finally, it might also be reckoned by readers that although it is about humor that this is not a funny book. That determination has finally to be left to the reader but the primary intent is not to be funny. But nor is it to be unfunny or boring. In books on humor comment is typically made about the level of humor in writings about humor. It has frequently been observed that much writing on humor is humorless (Terry Eagleton says

---

6. Lorenz, *On Aggression*, 283–84.

that Schopenhauer, who wrote a philosophy of humor, "is a thinker so unremittingly gloomy that his work, quite unintentionally, represents one of the great comic masterpieces of Western thought"!)[7] but my reckoning is that more recent writings are generally written with a lightness not typical of scholarly writing. A problem can emerge if the humor that is included takes over. One book I was reading clearly identified all examples of humor, whether paraphrases or quotations, in indented paragraphs making it so easy to pick them out that I found I was skipping from one humorous story to another without reading anything about the undoubtedly helpful observations that were being made about them in the author's discussion. One may ask, however, why we should think that someone writing about humor ought to be funny. Does someone writing about football have to be a good footballer? Or someone writing about music have to be a good musician? It could be that that having a direct and personal knowledge of the subject is a help, but we generally do not insist on it. Anyway, entertainment is not the primary aim. If that is what you want then go and get a joke book or a humorous novel.

In the next chapter there is a mapping out of the territory to be covered and a somewhat more detailed account of what will be involved in this study of humor. But before going there you might like to undertake a little exercise of your own. One that is, in a sense, the reverse of the opening illustration about Sue, which illustrates something of the range of humor that there is in life. Spend some time imagining a world *without humor of any kind*. Gradually eliminate all forms of humor, not only the more overt forms of entertainment and jokes and funny stories, but make sure you remove from your conception of the world all paradox, and incongruity; remind yourself that the oddest situation or person is not to be considered amusing in any way; make sure there is no joy and no interior amusement; and there are certainly no smiles and definitely no laughter. Now ask yourself, Is this a good world? How much joy is there here? How important is humor and laughter? Would I ever be prepared to live this way? And then move on to the next chapter.

---

7. Eagleton, *The Meaning of Life*, 82.

2

Mapping the Theo-Comical Territory

Humor is, in fact, a prelude to faith;
and laughter is the beginning of prayer.

—Reinhold Niebuhr[1]

It is widely understood that it is futile to attempt to explain a joke to someone who does not get it. E. B. White's quip is often paraphrased in support: "Explaining a joke is like dissecting a frog; it can be done but the frog dies in the process."[2] Of course, those who see this as an overgeneralization are probably right as sometimes explanations are necessary and successful, but it is still a useful point to make: explanations of humor are inherently difficult.

The difficulty involved in explaining specific instances of humor is not just due to *incidental factors*, such as the need to explain, for example, the double meaning of words or the cultural assumptions of certain people. It is actually directly connected to the less widely known *theoretical principle*, on which virtually all philosophers, psychologists, sociologists, and other theorists of humor agree, that there has never been any completely satisfactory overall, theoretical definition of humor. Humor is, in

---

1. Niebuhr, *Discerning the Signs*, 111.

2. The proper quote is "Humor can be dissected, as a frog can, but the thing dies in the process and the innards are discouraging to any but the pure scientific mind." White and White, *A Subtreasury of American Humor*, xvii. And the point about humor that is being made is not undermined, as it has been claimed, by the very earnest, technically correct, and somewhat humorless observation that the analogy is flawed because frogs are already dead before scientific dissection takes place.

principle, a somewhat elusive quality of life and while one cannot definitively rule out the possible development of some future theory that would comprehensively explain humor, it seems (given the attention that has already been paid to it) that it is not unreasonable to assume that humor has a fundamentally inexplicable dimension to it, similar to the fundamental uncertainty involved in quantum mechanics with regard to the simultaneous knowledge of both position and momentum of a specific particle. The uncertainty principle asserts that the more precisely one knows one of them then one necessarily knows less about the other. This indeterminacy is not the result of the considerable practical difficulties involved in measuring these properties but a theoretical uncertainty that can never be overcome (though it is a characteristic that can be used to advantage). As Gerald Bessière notes with regard to humor, "Humor has never allowed itself to be confined within a definition. It has always treated itself with humor."[3] Indeed, the closer one comes to defining the characteristics of humor the less funny it all is. Humor, it seems, requires a certain mystery and a degree of absurdity for its very existence.

Consider the fact that if one had a definitive, scientifically valid theory of humor in general then it would be possible to use that theory to predict certain outcomes in the application of humor. That is, one could know for certain, given knowledge of the circumstances, whether a joke would be seen as funny by particular people. One would know whether a certain quip would cause offense and whether a specific comment would be seen as ironic rather than as simply insulting. As it is, no one can do this with certainty. Some humorists obviously have a better sense of this than others but no one is right all the time. The reader may consider for themselves whether they think that such knowledge will ever be possible. As for myself I doubt that it will happen, and after saying as much as I believe needs be said about humor theologically in this volume, I may write a science fiction novel about humor in a world where, after much scientific research a theory is developed which can infallibly understand the thought processes and intentions behind all ironic, witty, and humorous comments and know with certainty what will, and will not, amuse (or depress, frustrate, or anger) people. It would be interesting to explore the ramifications of this and it might well explain the benefits involved in humor actually being an elusive phenomenon! Indeed, it will be shown later that this mysterious element has a distinctly theological dimension to it. Not that all theology

3. Bessière, "Humour," 81.

is mysterious or paradoxical—there is much that is theological which is plain and straightforward—but Christian theology, founded as it is on the incarnation, the cross, and the resurrection of Christ, is nonetheless deeply permeated with the mystery of God become man, the paradox of the death of the divine, and the promise of resurrection life.

What follows now are seven preliminary distinctions that will refine our understanding of humor because although it has been argued that precise and comprehensive definition is unlikely this does not mean that the concept cannot be more helpfully known by a process of clarification.

Humor as comedy rather than tragedy

Dante completed his epic narrative poem about a journey through purgatory, hell, and heaven, originally called simply *Comedia*, around 1320. For obvious reasons related to the content the title subsequently attracted the additional adjective, *Divine*, which, in the modern era is more easily understood as part of the title than "comedy," because there seems to be very little that is funny about a serious discussion of hell. But the point becomes clear when it is noted that in the fourteenth century "comedy" referred to (a) dramatic writings in the vernacular—the ordinary, daily language of life (rather than in classical Latin which, being somewhat removed from the hurly-burly of everyday life, was considered better suited for serious themes), which (b) finished well, with joy and laughter. If it did not—if it finished badly—then it was a tragedy. Humor does, indeed, belong to everyday life (it is often very "common" or even crude) and it always finishes well, so that all may laugh. In humor as in eschatology it is the finish that is important. The process of telling the story or the joke may not be humorous at all (although it can be) but if it finishes with a laugh then it is comedy (indeed, so much the better if the joyful ending comes as something of a surprise). Life can be like that. Dante's account, written in Tuscan (which partly because of the influence of the *Divine Comedy* became the standard Italian language) is a common language and robust account of the Christian view of life's destiny and as such it reflects the nature of the gospel story and the earthiness of the incarnation. But, crucially, it ends well, not with the laughter of trivial amusement or a temporary diversion but with the laughter that emerges from a joyful celebration of God's final victory. It is a comic vision of the world, one that does not despair at the incongruities, the frailty and the sinfulness of humanity, but which believes profoundly in God, eternal light and love, who will, one day, be all in all (1 Cor 15:28).

The laughter of God in heaven is no trivial or light-weight amusement. Instead, it is the eternal, whole-hearted laughter of one who has not merely overcome the pretensions of those who have opposed his grace and love ("The One enthroned in heaven laughs; the Lord scoffs at them"— Ps 2:4.) but who has instituted a new order of life ("They will enter Zion with singing; everlasting joy will crown their heads. Gladness and joy will overtake them, and sorrow and sighing will flee away." (Isa 35:10—see Rev 21:1–5). But it is not only the *ending* that is different; firm hope in God's ultimate success influences *present* life as well. A "comedy" may well involve tragedy but the point is that disaster is not allowed to ultimately control life. In this way the book of Job is, in the classic sense, a comedy. In fact, it is also a comedy in the more modern sense of the word, but that is the subject of a later chapter.

The implication of this "comic" approach is that the story is able to embrace complex life patterns. The comic is playful as well as serious and not fixated, as tragic figures often are, on single perceptions of life. Comedy can cope with (and laugh at) ambiguity and complexity, and can have open endings. In classical tragedy these fixations (on duty, revenge, self-pity or power) lead people with dreadful certainty towards their self-imposed fate. The comic, who can laugh at all things—sometimes even the apparently tragic—may appear to have become unnaturally detached from socially correct and psychologically appropriate feelings, but this specific, humorous form of detachment is actually the result of a clearer picture of the incongruities and frailty of human life and of the faithfulness of God. The true comic is not just playing everything for easy laughs but is, much more seriously, the one who knows the God of the future. A genuinely comic view of life includes (a) an understanding that laughter in times of sadness, such as bereavement, is not inappropriate and is often helpful; (b) a somewhat ironic view of social and political life, not believing that everything depends on the results of the next election or the behavior of politicians or other important people; (c) an attitude that avoids over-seriousness and any fixation that make it impossible to laugh at oneself. In theological terms the comic view of life is an act of faith.

MAPPING THE THEO-COMICAL TERRITORY

Humor as ancient and modern

The main point of the previous discussion concerns the fundamentally comic dimension of life, but it also demonstrates the way in which the meaning of words and concepts changes over time. One has to avoid reducing the language and thought of the past to the conventions and theories of the present. A major issue is that "comedy" in common contemporary thought, more than was previously the case, relates to a much less consequential and much more specific phenomenon relating to being amused. Certain other aspects of the more ancient understandings of laughter and humor will be discussed later but it should be noted at this point that as far as the English language is concerned that prior to the eighteenth century the word "humor" (or "humour") did not mean "funny." Consequently, earlier discussions of that which is amusing tended to focus upon laughter[4] while the concept of humor was used more broadly, concerning what we would call temperament. This was derived from the father of medicine, Hippocrates (c. 460–370 BC), who held that a balance between four humors or bodily fluids (blood, phlegm, black and yellow bile) was responsible for good health. This was foundational for ancient medicine. Later, Galen (c. 130–200 BC) developed humoral theory by suggesting that there are four basic temperaments (sanguine, phlegmatic, choleric, and melancholic) associated with these humors and an excess or deficiency of one or other would cause, for example, irritability, anger, or depression. Humoral theory thus connects the physical with the psychological, though one should not race too far ahead and infuse it with all the assumptions and the conclusions of modern psychology. The ancient meaning of humor as a reference to bodily fluids and their related temperament was still prominent in 1598 when the English playwright Ben Jonson produced his well-known comedy *Every Man in His Humour*, in which every character is dominated by one or other of the humors such that, as Jonson said, "it doth draw all his affects, spirits, and his powers, in their conflictions, all to run one way, this may be truly said to be a humour."[5] Characters are stereotypically strict, witty, flippant, pretentious, and so forth. The meaning of humor only began to change with this closer connection between humor and the way that exaggerated humors can be amusing, beginning around the time of Jonson's comedy.

4. Morreall, "Philosophy and Religion," 211.
5. Jonson, *Every Man in His Humour*, 103–9.

The essential point here is the need to be aware of the historical context of humor theory and practice. There is, for example, a growth in understanding of the relationship between humorous event and underlying temperament. Humor will never be understood solely in terms of events, words, and actions—it is as much a quality of the person who has, in some form or another, "a sense of humor"—and our understanding of this has changed over time. In modern Western thought humor has been psychologized—primarily understood in terms of psychological categories and this has been both incredibly insightful and, at the same time, potentially limiting.

Humor as cultural and universal

Humor is undoubtedly both universal and significantly influenced in its specific form by culture. Cultural factors include the influence of gender, family relationships, and social expectations. Research in Western culture has produced conflicting evidence on gender differences in humor, although a majority of studies support the notion of there being a difference. Many aspects of humor are consistent for males and females but (a) there are differences regarding attitudes to humor about gender differences; (b) there appears to be a greater female appreciation of nonsense or absurd humor; (c) men are more likely to utilize aggressive humor; and (d) women are more likely to employ self-deprecation, understatement, and irony.[6]

In regard to family relationships one of the primary questions concerns who one can appropriately joke with and what topics are suitable. Acceptable and non-acceptable joking relationships vary with culture, and research on non-industrial societies shows this is influenced by the nature of the relationship, marriage customs, sexual taboos, and the level of intimacy involved. On the one hand it may be completely inappropriate to joke either at all or in regard to certain topics with specific categories of relative while, on the other hand, certain relationships may involve very specific possibilities for humor (such as the possibility of occasions where one may appropriately and humorously throw excrement at certain cousins).[7] Outside family relationships the level of friendship is the most important

---

6. The issue may sometimes be influenced by a degree of gender bias in the research methods employed where studies utilize humor created by males, or lack equal numbers of male and females. Roeckelein, *The Psychology of Humor*, 238–39.

7. Palmer, *Taking Humor Seriously*, 13.

prerequisite for establishing a joking relationship. In industrial societies family relationships are important but social and professional groupings are also significant regulators of appropriate humor.[8] The form humor takes is also an important determinant of social acceptability. Humorous, rather than offensive, intent is frequently signaled by phrases such as, "Did you hear the one about . . ." Indeed, the joke has been an informal definition of humor. In a very loose, popular way humor is defined as telling jokes. This is seen in some responses to the admission that one is writing a book about humor—some are confused and wonder why a theologian is writing a joke book. The joke—in its various forms (riddle, pun, knock-knock, shaggy-dog story, punch-line jokes, etc.)—is certainly cultural in form and will go through various trends and cycles.

These and other factors are part of overall cultural approaches to humor. In general, Western culture perceives humor as a natural feature of life and a positive disposition that is widely possessed. It is reckoned to enhance health, promote creativity, strengthen coping, encourage self-actualization, and enhance social relationships. Those with a sense of humor are seen as positive and attractive in both social and work-related contexts. Those who lack a sense of humor are seen more negatively. By contrast, Chinese culture views humor as a more controversial disposition in social interactions and possessed (largely) by specialists in humor. This is related to the Confucian tradition, which encourages restraint in laughter to demonstrate dignity and social formality. Moderation in laughter, as in all things, is expected because it expresses extreme emotion and one has to be serious to be respected. Confucian concerns for maintaining proper social order and hierarchy means that humor is only appropriate at certain times, in conjunction with certain subjects, and only with certain people. A modest smile is preferred to hilarious laughter.

Cultural variations in regard to humor can produce confusing issues in translation and cross-cultural understanding. Languages and cultures do not all categorize humor in the same way and so one has to be wary. Freud's notable *Jokes and their Relation to the Unconscious* has "jokes"— translating *witz*—but it can also mean ingenuity or wit.[9] Freud distinguishes *witz* from *scherz*, which can be jest or hoax, and given that the conceptual clarity of his threefold classification of humor into joke, comic, and mimetic forms is debated anyway, translation issues have the potential for making it less

---

8. Apte, *Humor and Laughter*, 65–66.
9. Palmer, *Taking Humour Seriously*, 6.

clear. The situation is by no means unique to Freud and, given that to some extent terminology creates understanding, rather than merely expressing it, care has to be taken in cultural interpretation.

This can be connected with Christian theological thought which, of course, is familiar with the difficulties involved in relating the universal and the culturally particular. It is not a general, abstract, theoretical philosophy, for God is known through specific incarnation as a Jewish male in what we now refer to as the first century. The knowledge of God and the knowledge of humanity are thus intimately tied together. One cannot understand human nature apart from the incarnate Christ. The universal aspect of human nature is only experienced and known specifically. It is not expressed other than through particular cultural form. In biblical terms the human person is primarily defined by the *imago dei*—a concept that far outweighs the brevity of scriptural references to it. It is a term that references both the created order (Gen 1:27) and the eschatological future involved in humanity being incorporated into Christ (Col 1:15–20; 3:10; 2 Cor 4:4; Jas 3:8–10; Eph 4:20–24; Heb 1:3). The universality of humor, as an essential aspect of the person, is connected with the *imago dei*. To be human is to be humorous and this humor is, along with all aspects of the person, to be redeemed and a part of the future eschatological life.

Humor as event and temperament

People often refer to a situation as being humorous but although there usually is some definable aspect of incongruity in the situation that leads to the humor the ultimate determinant of humor lies in the individual's perception: it is funny (or ironic, amusing, witty, and so forth) because they believe it to be so. The nature of the two dimensions of humor—that which lies in the situation and the perception of it—will be considered further later but it should be noted here that both need to be considered. Incongruity in the event is a necessary but not in itself a sufficient condition for humor.

The subjective dimension of humor is sometimes seen as an emotion. It has certainly been noted that humor, and especially laughter, has the effect of *blocking* emotions. One has to temporarily leave other feelings behind when one laughs with other people. Is this humorous experience something that blocks emotions or itself an emotion? Most commonly, humor has been described as a feeling or emotion, though some have seen it negatively (malice according to Plato, hatred according to Spinoza), and others more positively (commonly as amusement or delight) or, sometimes, as an even more elusive emotion. Hobbes described it as "the passion that [hitherto] hath no name," although he goes on to describe it as a form of joy arising from a sense of superiority (which is not exactly what is involved in genuine joy according to many other people). Wallace Chafe says that there is an underlying emotion, for which we have no agreed word though he sees it as a form of non-seriousness, not being earnest, a lightness of being which may produce laughter.[10] The ancient notion of *eutrapelia* (used notably by Aristotle and Aquinas) to describe this feeling will, in a later chapter, be a useful resource.

The notion of humor specifically as an emotion rather than as, say, "a cognitive experience," has been defended by Robert Sharpe, who notes seven similarities between humor and the emotions. Humor has, for example, a distinction between the subject and the object of their emotion, there are degrees of humor and emotion, and humor can be cultivated, just as one can learn to love someone.[11] But the notion of humor as an emotion has also been challenged by John Morreall, who observes that, unlike emotions, humor involves no set of beliefs or desires and produces no practical response. The physiological processes that take place do not, of themselves, demonstrate that humor is an emotion.[12] Whether technically an emotion or not (and there are both similarities and differences compared with the standard emotions) the subjective dimension of humor is a personal quality or attribute, a way of being, or as it is commonly said, a "sense" that one has. This perception is essential and also more mysterious, more difficult to explain, and it relates to the individual temperament of the person. What kind of sense of humor do they have? A comic temperament is one that is likely to more readily perceive the significance of life's many incongruities. It is possible to temporarily be "in a good humor" but there is also an underlying temperament involving having "a sense of humor" of some kind that is characteristic of the person.

Theologically speaking, what is of interest here is not the temperament or sense of humor that treats every part of life as a joke, as a means of finding a pun, a laugh, or an appreciation from others—that is a mechanical, utilitarian approach to humor that does not, of itself, go to any depth in comprehending God, the world, oneself or others. Having a mature

---

10. Chafe, *The Importance of Not Being Earnest*, 1.
11. Sharpe, "Seven Reasons Why Amusement is an Emotion."
12. Morreall, "Philosophy and Religion," 235–46.

sense of humor does not mean being good at developing jokes, but rather is about having a particular approach to life. This may mean observing the unintended irony involved in certain political statements; being alert to satire; being able to find joy and laughter in the midst of the most difficult circumstances; being amused by the most simple daily situations in life; being provoked to action by the incongruity—and injustice—of certain events; being better able to understand and forgive the foibles and frailties of others. It does not mean not being serious about life but it does mean being more playful; it means coming closer to others through friendship and appreciation of others despite, and perhaps because, of shared humor; it means being appreciative, rather than despairing of the world; and, altogether it means understanding that, despite appearances to the contrary, joyfulness and not tragedy is the final outcome of all things. This temperament, this sense of humor, is part and parcel of the life of faith, hope, love, and especially joy.

Humor as mockery and joy

To some people it may be strange and confronting to say that humor involves both joy and mockery, but it is only our modern, culturally based view of humor and laughter that finds mockery to be not very funny. Some people definitely prefer humor to be nice and well-behaved; others prefer a more controversial approach and welcome humor that is prepared to really make fun of people although it is usually reckoned to be socially inappropriate to make fun of people on the basis of race or disability. Politicians and others figures usually reckoned to have power and prestige are, however, often considered fair game. But there are limits, even for politicians. Perhaps the exceptions are terrorists, although this immediately brings to mind the fact that the most controversial humor in recent years has focused upon humor directed at terrorists, or is it at their religion? Those objecting to various cartoons and satirical articles have not only been terrorists themselves but those who have interpreted the humor as an attack on the religion itself, which it may—or may not—have been.

God, however, has no compunction about mocking some people and laughing to scorn those who are wicked, both individuals ("the Lord laughs at the wicked, for he knows their day is coming," Ps 37:13) and nations ("But you laugh at them, Lord; you scoff at all those nations," Ps 59:8). In the light of this how are we to assess whether there is humor in

Mary's song at the news that she was to bear a child by the Holy Spirit? The Magnificat of Luke 1:46–55 is a song of praise that glorifies the Lord for the great things he has done. It is often seen as a hymn of liberation because it stresses the way in which God does mighty deeds in scattering those who are proud and powerful. Would those who were under Roman rule who heard this hymn have laughed at the declaration that rulers would be brought down from their thrones and the humble lifted high? A theology of humor needs to take such things into account in understanding both divine and human humor.

Humor as amusement and wisdom

No definition of humor can avoid observing that humor is amusing, but it can also be the means of enabling significant insights into character, social situations, and politics. Discussions of humor from the seventeenth to the twentieth century typically distinguished between humor and wit, although the dividing line was not always clear-cut. Humor was more related to outright laughter and was more positive, more physical, more earthy, and more suited to the lower classes. Wit was more intellectual, more gentlemanly, sharper, and more challenging in its observations. Freud held this distinction and then added a third category of non-verbal slapstick, which he termed "the comic." It is often assumed that it is intellectual wit which is the more able to impart wisdom but the effect of simpler forms of humor that are perhaps more physical than intellectual in orientation should not be overlooked. The physical responses to simpler forms of humor vary from vigorous belly-laughs through various more restrained forms of laughter and chuckling to assorted smiles and grins. There are also many occasions where no physical response is apparent. The more extreme forms of response actually sound like an illness. People temporarily lose control of their voice (they laugh involuntarily and sometimes can't stop, possibly embarrassing themselves), and may also uncontrollably twitch their head or arms or even their whole bodies, they may engage in a form of crying, may breathe abnormally heavily, and may need to sit down, as though in physical distress. It is possible to "laugh till it hurts." And yet people enjoy it immensely.

Nonetheless, sometimes, indeed, perhaps frequently, there is little observable by way of physical response. But that does not mean that a person is not amused or that they do not find in the situation some absurdity, incongruity, or insight that is not only amusing but which gives them a deeper understanding of some aspect of life. Comic situations can impart wisdom and understanding as well as amusement. While writing this I am watching the current series of the Australian satirical comedy *Utopia*, in which public servants in the fictitious National Building Authority are charged with developing projects to enhance the national infrastructure ("nation building—one white elephant at a time"). In the offices of the NBA office politics and incompetence challenge efficiency. The competent leaders of the organization, Tony and Nat are constantly thwarted by inefficiency, obsession with new systems that take more time than they are worth, office socialization, political interference, and sheer incompetence (often well meaning). If anything is achieved it is by the least competent. Even when one does not laugh out loud the comic situations—which are not always so outlandish that they cannot be believed—not only make it one of the funniest (and currently most awarded) programs but one that gives insight and understanding regarding human relationships, organizational structures, and political constraints. Humor is not only amusement, it can be a form of wisdom.

Even more significantly humor can be the means of imparting spiritual wisdom and insight. The extent, the nature and the use of humor in Scripture will be discussed more fully in a later chapter. So it will be sufficient here to note, as one example, that there are pedagogical similarities between the parables of Jesus and the humor of *Utopia*. The parables are their own literary form (just as much as a TV script) and the parable of the unforgiving servant (Matt 18:23–35) similarly has droll humor that enables the communication of a serious message. The story begins with a king calling to account and threatening to imprison a man who owes him 10,000 talents. Now that is an amount that would make those listening to the parable stop and think about what was going on and how they might react, because that is an amount equivalent to 60 million days' wages and it represents more money than there was in circulation in a sizeable country like Egypt in the first century.[13] One can imagine the listeners grinning even before the story goes further, but it then has the desperate servant preposterously declaring, presumably with a straight face, "Be patient with me and I will pay back everything"! The parable is presenting a serious situation in a very comic form.

---

13. Keener, *Bible Background Commentary*, 92.

The king unexpectedly forgives the entire debt and releases the servant who immediately goes and demands repayment of a debt owed to him by another servant. The amount he is owed is trivial and stands in sharp contrast to the massive amount he has been forgiven, but despite that he is unable to show the same grace as the king and has the man who cannot pay him thrown into prison. Listeners would be aware of the irony involved here, would be likely to think "Yes, I know a &#@*# like that!" They may well then laugh heartily at the king's subsequent judgement on the unforgiving servant—that he be imprisoned and tortured until he repays his massive debt—which, of course, would make that even more of an impossibility! Only after all this would the listeners realize that they have been led into a trap as their righteous laughter at the punishment of the unforgiving servant is turned back on themselves as Jesus draws out his intended message, "This is how my heavenly Father will treat *you* unless you forgive your brother or sister from your heart." One hopes that they can then laugh at themselves being impaled on Jesus' teaching because if they are unable to do that then they will learn nothing about forgiveness. Gaining wisdom and insight without a sense of humor is difficult, if not impossible.

Humor as sinful and virtuous

While it will be strongly argued here that a good sense of humor is spiritually beneficial and theologically appropriate it must be recognized that certain forms and uses of humor are inappropriate and that some laughter is sinful. As it will be shown later, the Christian tradition has developed a long list of objections to humor. It has been seen as offensive, aggressive, excluding, irresponsible, hedonistic, mocking, undignified, frivolous, spiteful, madness, anarchic, unworthy of God, and foolish. Despite all this, humor and laughter should be seen as gifts from God. They are gifts that can be misused and abused but they are gifts nonetheless. The epistle of James points out that "out of the same mouth come praise and cursing" (3:10). Cursing is wrong but it does not detract from the goodness of the praise of God. The one who is wise should show wisdom by their good life and the way that they speak. So too with humor, people should demonstrate the moral benefits of humor rather than the morally unhelpful ones. Humor is, in fact, an important quality for those who wish to be spiritually mature. It may even be described as a virtue although not in quite the same way as other virtues, such as those described in Galatians as the fruit of the Spirit—love, joy, peace, patience, kindness, goodness, faithfulness, and self-control.

The difference lies in the way the virtues and other qualities are categorized. Kindness, for example, is, by definition always good. Humor, on the other hand, is not always morally right. However, the difference is not great, as it is simply the result of nomenclature because the qualities that produce kindness can also be distorted to produce that which is not good (for example, generosity and help shown to people who are known to use their resources to abuse others). In that case, however, such generosity would not be referred to as kindness and so that virtue escapes all blame for the action, whereas humor has to bear the opprobrium that comes from its misuse. The reality, however, is that *any* human quality can be perverted and in that regard humor is no different to kindness or the other virtues.

The real question then is whether humor is actually a good in itself, or whether it is only good as a means of achieving some other end such as wisdom, joy, or patience. It is argued here that there is a both/and relationship between virtue and humor. Humor is, on the one hand, an important means by which one can enhance the life of virtue generally. It is a disposition or quality of life that enables the exercise of virtues such as love, faith, and hope. On the other hand, humor is also a virtue in itself, not unlike the traditional four cardinal virtues of justice, temperance, courage, and prudence. These four virtues when combined with the three principal theological virtues of faith, hope, and love make up the seven heavenly virtues of Christian tradition. The categorization is somewhat arbitrary and should not be seen to separate these virtues from myriad other biblical and other virtues. If a virtue is simply a habitual and firm disposition to do good then one could, on the basis of biblical material alone, reckon there to be over a hundred.

The traditional reckoning that there are cardinal virtues as well as theological ones points to the fact that life is lived as a whole and that there are myriad qualities and dispositions that are necessary in order for one to demonstrate virtues such as faith, hope, and love. Hope may be enhanced by temperance or restraint, love in difficult circumstances may requires courage, and faith may well need a good sense of justice to be kept strong. Similarly, there are many situations where humor is essential for a life of virtue. Indeed, although the tradition of the church has shockingly neglected it, humor is an essential part of the virtuous life. Life cannot be lived well without a sense of humor.

Although Scripture does not nominate humor as a virtue it is an important disposition and not merely in a utilitarian sense. In the Christian life means and ends are closely correlated and a sense of humor (being much more than the ability to make jokes) as part of one's attitude towards life not only enhances life in the present and contributes towards one's growth to maturity, it is an important dimension of one's ultimate relationship with others and with God. It is intimately connected with a joyfully lived life, it is an expression of hope that God is in control and will draw all things to himself, and it is part of the life of faith. Reinhold Niebuhr said that "humor is, in fact, a prelude to faith; and laughter is the beginning of prayer."[14]

---

14. Niebuhr, *Discerning the Signs*, 111.

3

Jesus the Laugh-Maker

If we did not know all His retorts by heart,
if we had not taken the sting out of them by incessant repetition . . .
we should reckon Him among the greatest wits of all time.

—Dorothy L. Sayers[1]

Did you hear the one about the wealthy farmer who invited all his neighbors to a great banquet at his house? There was a famous chef preparing the food and there was entertainment and everything. They were all coming but then, at the last minute, one of them called and said, "Look, I'm really sorry but I've just acquired some new land and I want to go and check it out, so I'm afraid I cannot come." Then, soon after that, a second one called and said, "Look, I'm really sorry but I've just bought a new tractor and I want to go and try it out, so I'm afraid I cannot come." Then, soon after that, a third one called and said, "Look, I'm really sorry but I've just got married and I really want to go and . . . well, anyway, I'm afraid I cannot come."

This, of course, is a contemporary version of the Lord Jesus' parable of the Great Banquet (Luke 14:15–24), a parable that is as much a comic tale as the parable of the unforgiving servant who owed the king more than the entire budget of Egypt (referred to in chapter 2). The danger with this sort of retelling, of course, is that of imposing humor where none was intended. It is possible to make *any* story funny by adding or distorting elements. So was the original a comic tale with a serious point, or just a serious account of an everyday situation with which Jesus could make his point? It has, in fact, all the hallmarks of humor. In this parable a clear pattern of excuse is

---

1. Sayers, *The Man Born to be King*, 26.

established by the first two (involving identical terminology and structure) and involves:

a. a statement about a new acquisition (land or oxen/tractor), followed by
b. an expression of a desire to see it or try it out, and then
c. the apologetic conclusion, "I cannot come."

Not only is a pattern established in the first two excuses but their unusual nature point towards a potentially humorous situation by raising questions for the one listening to, or reading it. The man buys a property (or ox or a tractor) and then goes to look at it (or test it)? Most people do that before they buy. So this seems strange. And if they have also seen and checked their goods prior to purchase then why the rush to do it again now and miss the big banquet? Are these excuses arising from the fact that they really don't want to be at the meal? Do they have something against the wealthy farmer?

Then, significantly, although the third man's excuse is phrased in exactly the same form of words as the first two responses the second part of the response is omitted. There is simply:

a. a statement of acquisition ("I have just married") followed by
c. the apologetic conclusion ("I cannot come").

There is nothing that parallels the excuses, ("I want to see it" or "I want to test it"), although it is possible that in the original oral tradition a pregnant pause could well have been included in between the two, allowing the audience to figure out for themselves exactly what it is that the newly married man wants to go and see or try out. As Richard Longenecker says we should not think that "this involves an eagerness to taste the wife's cooking or assess her cleaning skills . . . or to discover her intellectual acumen by discussing current events with her. Clearly the third invitee is eager simply to enjoy the sexual delights of married life with his new wife."[2] And so, with that, although Jesus may not be described as laughing himself, he has certainly got his listeners smiling—and perhaps also wondering whether this marriage (or the other acquisitions) is something that has genuinely arisen recently or whether it is simply an excuse to avoid an invitation the guest does not want.

2. Longenecker, "Humorous Jesus?" 188–89.

Longenecker is sure that "the reason that the witty feature of Luke's version of this parable needs to be explicated is that, in our predominantly print cultures, we have lost our sensitivity to the kind of structural patterning and rhetorical delivery that was elementary to discourse in the predominantly oral cultures of antiquity."[3] The 3 + 1 structure (of three problems and a resolution) is a time-honored principle of oral story-telling in many cultures, including Jewish folklore, and it appears in other parables.[4] All of this creates a situation where the amused audience is now, unbeknownst to them, in a better position to be challenged by the unexpected conclusion:

> In the end none of his neighbors came and the wealthy farmer was pretty angry about this and so he went into town and invited all the homeless and poor people he could find and brought them to his house to enjoy the food and the entertainment. "None of those who were invited need bother turning up," he declared. "They will never get anything from me."

Suddenly the humor has a purpose, a challenge one for anyone saying that they are ready to accept Jesus' invitation to discipleship. This becomes very clear when this story is seen in the context of the words of Jesus immediately following this. There is the cryptic and challenging statement about followers needing to "hate father and mother, wife and children" if they wish to be his disciple, the warning implicit in the stories of the builder and the king who do not count the cost before commencing either to build or to wage war, and the statement about salt that eventually loses its saltiness and thus is fit for nothing. This is challenging teaching and, as Jesus concludes, "Whoever has ears to hear, let them hear."

Too little laughter

Listening attentively to Scripture to discern the significance of humor can, initially at least, be surprisingly difficult, although as one's ears attune to the humor that is present it becomes progressively easier. One has to be open in attitude and, given the important role Scripture typically plays in people's lives, there can be a lot to overcome in establishing the right sense

---

3. Ibid., 184.

4. Ibid., 186–87, which cites H. Schwartz, *Elijah's Violin and Other Jewish Folktales*, a collection of folktales from a wide variety of locations over a significant time scale, in which the basic pattern is repeated with an almost predictable regularity. Also see, for example, the parable of the sower in Mark 4:3–8, 13–20; Matt 13:3–8, Luke 8:4–8, 11–15.

of a passage. Thus there are a number of factors that inhibit a comic reading of Scripture. It is sometimes assumed that sacred Scripture must be taken seriously and therefore that it cannot appropriately contain humor. Because Scripture is, in Christian orthodoxy, a sacred, infallible, authoritative text concerning the most serious issues pertaining to salvation it is sometimes assumed that it could not be funny. The inclusion of books into the canon of Scripture is certainly controlled by the way they contribute to revealing the overarching story of creation and redemption, and as every Christian knows there is significant stress on the passion narrative in the Gospels. In reality the "seriousness" or significance of salvation is not contrary to the joy or laughter that are essential to both God and humanity. An inability to perceive humor or lightness, irony or parody may influence one's capacity to fully understand Jesus. Unfortunately, the constant repetition of existing patterns of church behavior can inculcate approaches to faith that treat humor with exaggerated caution. It has been reckoned that "if we did not know all His retorts by heart, if we had not taken the sting out of them by incessant repetition in the accents of the pulpit, . . . we should reckon Him among the greatest wits of all time."[5]

It is also the case that the nature of humor can be understood too narrowly. Humor is not only about jokes or laughter, it also involves much gentler forms of humor such as lightness of expression, irony, whimsy, drollery, and leg-pulling. Although demonstrating, as I have done above, that there is actual comic material in the parables shows that humor is present, it can have the disadvantage of reinforcing the notion that humor is only about getting laughs from amusing situations. Once one is aware of the possibility of humor one can become more attuned to other, more sensitive references that are intended subtly. Unfortunately, some studies only operate in a proof-texting manner, making reference only to parts of Scripture that make explicit reference to laughter. This can result in two problems. The first is that *too much* can be made of the few references that there are by claiming that they show that God has a sense of humor. For example, passages such as Psalms 2:4, 37:13, and 59:8 all involve the Lord laughing, but it is actually a case of God scoffing at the wicked, which is hardly a demonstration of the kind of humor usually under discussion. The second problem is that the search for humor can too easily lead to the conclusion that there is very little that Scripture contributes to this topic. It has been argued, for example, that there is not a single (real) joke in the Bible; that

---

5. Sayers, *The Man Born to be King*, 26.

laughter is always an expression of scorn; that no saint, prophet, or apostle is ever spoken of as laughing; and that Jesus wept but never laughed. A. N. Whitehead is often quoted in this regard: "The total absence of humor from the bible is one of the most singular things in all literature."[6] Nietzsche wished that Jesus "had remained in the wilderness and far from the good and just (*who crucified him*)! Perhaps he would have learnt to live and love the earth—and laughter too."[7] Reinhold Niebuhr asserted that the Bible is virtually devoid of humor.[8] In short there is a long-standing tradition that humor has very little place in Scripture. It extends back to the early fathers of the church who found little laughter in Scripture and often assumed that it had no worthwhile place in the Christian community.

The absence of descriptions of Christ laughing may be connected with the fact that as early as the fourth century a number of writers including the historian Eusebius and the church leader and theologian Augustine observed that there were no known records or other reliable recollections of the Lord's personal appearance. Recording his appearance does not appear to have been of primary concern to the early church, and this is perhaps consistent with the fact that reference was occasionally made to the prophecy in Isaiah 53:2, "he had no beauty or majesty to attract us to him." But as the church itself grew to be an important part of society, increasing in power and prosperity, the notion of modest bearing underwent a change and by the middle ages Christ took on an allegedly handsome appearance that was thought to be more in keeping with his status. One of the main sources for this was the Epistle of Lentulus, which describes Christ as of medium upright stature, with wavy hair flowing over his shoulders, smooth skin, a slightly reddish complexion, faultless nose and mouth, an abundant beard, bright eyes, and beautiful hands and arms. Along with this testimony to his physical attractiveness was another observation—no doubt intended to contribute to this picture of the perfect man who redeemed the world—that he was often known to weep but never to laugh. This claim, however, is no more theologically reliable than the physical description it accompanies. "Fake news" has always been around and the fictitious Lentulus and his apocryphal epistle probably belong some time from the late eleventh to the

---

6. See Price, *Dialogues of Alfred North Whitehead*, 30, and Radday and Athalya, *On Humour and the Comic*, 21.

7. My parenthetical comment. Cited in Trueblood, *The Humor of Christ*, 15.

8. Niebuhr, *Discerning the Signs of the Times*, 111.

fourteenth century.[9] The epistle was a literary invention but it did, however, have its intended effect upon medieval piety, confirming existing perceptions of both Christ's beauty and his gravity. But the evidence that the epistle is an invention is found within the letter itself. Lentulus is alleged to have had what is in fact the non-existent position of governor of Jerusalem, and all local governors are known and there is no Lentulus among them. Moreover, if genuine it would have been addressed to the emperor not the senate, and it would not have reflected the Christian attitudes it contains. In short, it represents, at most, the belief of Christians in the middle ages that neither human nor divine perfection included laughter, a fact reinforced in all medieval images of Christ, none of which showed him smiling or laughing. This tradition that views Christ as humorless is still influential today in various parts of the Christian tradition such as some parts of the Orthodox ascetic and conservative evangelical tradition but, as we shall see, it no longer has the influence it once had. Biblical scholars have gradually been shifting the consensus of opinion about humor towards a greater recognition of its role for around 150 years.

Too much laughter

Renewed interest in the laughter of Christ is connected, in part, with modern rediscoveries of several non-canonical gnostic writings of the late second century which have descriptions of Jesus laughing. *The Gospel of Judas* describes Jesus laughing while breaking bread with his disciples and then again while discussing the future[10] with them, both instances in a relatively unremarkable way. However, in a very different mode, the Coptic *Apocalypse of Peter* describes Jesus laughing at the time of the crucifixion, but it relies on a view of Christ that is quite at odds with the orthodox view. This view of the crucifixion involves a distinction between Jesus of the flesh (who is crucified) and Jesus of the Spirit (who lives). In the apocalyptic vision to Peter the living Jesus says,

> He whom you see beside the tree glad and laughing, this is the living Jesus. But he into whose hands and feet they drive the nails is his fleshly (likeness), the "ransom," which (alone) they (are able

---

9. McClintock and Strong, eds., "Lentulus," 350.
10. Krosney, *The Lost Gospel*, 286.

to) put to shame. That came into being after his likeness. But look on him and on me![11]

The difference is clear. The physical likeness of Jesus is crucified and the living Jesus ("the bodiless Spirit, perceptible only spiritually") is able to laugh because he is set free and still lives. It has been reckoned in the past that the inclusion of references to Jesus laughing in the Gospels would have help make him more real and accessible, would have "humanized" him more, and, similarly, it has been suggested now that these references to his laughter in the apocryphal literature has the same effect. This can hardly be the case, however, when it involves the person of Jesus being divided in two with the purely spiritual, bodiless Jesus laughing at the crucifixion of his lesser, physical likeness. This involves the extraction of Jesus from the real, physical world that actual people inhabit. This is hardly an affirmation of humanity.

Jesus as the laugh-maker

One is left then, with the canonical Gospels, which lack any description of Jesus laughing. Clearly the New Testament Gospels do not see using humor in order to humanize Jesus as being important to their purpose. But then, the Gospels are not at all interested in describing *everything* about Jesus. It is often noted that they are not biographies in the sense in which we understand them today. There is, for example a huge focus upon the last week of Christ's life and significant portions of his life receive no attention at all. There is also a focus upon his role in salvation that involves a neglect of many aspects of his life. Moreover, while Jesus is not presented as one laughing *he is certainly the one who makes others laugh* in a wide variety of ways. His teaching is full of imagery that is associated with various forms of humor and the Gospels are presented in such a way that humor can be found in many places. The examples of Gospel humor given so far are only a part of the full story that is being rediscovered today. Terri Bednarz, for example, has tracked the status of humor through the various stages of the scholarly quest for the historical Jesus, extending from the first studies of biblical humor in the late nineteenth century through to the present day.

In the first period of the quest for the historical Jesus (defined as being from 1883 to 1906) the idea of humor was introduced into various

---

11. Schneemelcher, *New Testament Apocrypha*, 708–9.

discussions and was recognized as a necessary part of the humanity of Jesus. But there were also many objections to the notion of biblical humor, such as the claim that Jesus would not use the harsher forms of humor such as satire; and that while humor might have been used for didactic purposes it would not have been used for enjoyment. Nonetheless, the issue was now being discussed and in the early to middle twentieth century there were plenty of people who struggled with the older idea of a completely or relatively humorless Jesus. Bednarz notes that in the period of the second quest (1954–1979) there was some recognition of the way that humor could be utilized to explicate serious issues. The question of humor was also involved in the discussion of the relationship between the Jesus of history and the Christ of faith, and also about the role of editors in presenting material humorously. There was discussion about why it was so difficult to recognize humor and various types of humor (amusement, political, etc.) were identified. As the third quest (1980–2014) proceeded there was more focus on literary construction, plots, typologies, irony, satire, sarcasm, paradox, aphorisms, wit, caricature, and surprise reversals. These tended to be associated with Gospel authors.

This development of thought makes very clear the need to overcome the cultural gap which lies between the ancient Near East and modern Western culture. Humor is shaped by a wide range of sociocultural factors and frequently the whole point of humor is to point towards some incongruity that is based on very subtle literary, verbal, cultural, political, social, or gender definitions and distinctions. Humor is rarely identified ("This is a joke or a pun . . .") and identifying it requires close knowledge of the culture. Scholarly research has gone a long way towards identifying humor in Scripture and the findings concerning humor of the various stages of the quest for the historical Jesus are the result of shifting from examining the Bible as purely a descriptive, historical document (with brief references to laughter here and there) to seeing the Bible as a literary document that involves various types of humor in the way it is written. Apart from a number of descriptions of God's scorn for the wicked, the laughter of fools, and a few references to genuine joy and laughter the former approach produced very little. The latter approach demonstrates much more clearly the extent of humor throughout Scripture and classifies the various types. It needs to be supplemented by more considerations of the theological, philosophical, ethical, and spiritual dimensions of humor that emerge from this new understanding of humor within Scripture.

Being ready for humor

If the parables of the unforgiving servant who owes his boss ten billion dollars, and the wealthy farmer whose invitation to a banquet is rejected by a man who wants to get on with his honeymoon are any example then one should not be surprised if other parables are also humorous. And if more humor is discerned in the parables then perhaps other aspects of Jesus' life and teaching will be better illuminated by assuming a comic or at least a light-hearted attitude. What is important here, as has already been suggested concerning humor generally, is the critical importance of the attitude of the person who is interpreting the situation. Nothing is funny unless the person has reason to believe it ought to be so. An adult tripping and falling heavily to the ground is not amusing at all, unless the person observing this believes it ought to be funny (as when watching a comedy on TV). The significance of there being an expectation that something may contain humor is seen in the myriad verbal and literary ways that humor is flagged in advance (including the unsophisticated, "Did you hear the one about . . ." and the manner in which novels, films, or TV programs are titled and promoted). There is good reason for this, establishing a particular expectation in the mind of the audience is critically important for successful humor.

The importance of this subjective attitude became vividly clear recently when I was reading a poem that initially mystified me. It was in the *Penguin Anthology of Australian Poetry*, which I was gradually working my way through. I had read a number of stanzas in a particular poem but was having difficulty getting the sense of a poem that appeared to me to be a very serious but quite difficult to comprehend examination of life, until I noticed that it was by Ern Malley, at which point my understanding changed completely and I finished reading the poem with great amusement and outright laughter. This was because although I still had difficulty understanding the poem I did know that Malley was the fictitious central character of Australia's most well-known literary hoax (or simply "the greatest literary hoax of the twentieth century" if one believes American poet and editor David Lehman.)[12] Malley and his poems were created by James McAuley and Harold Stewart in order, as they saw it, to debunk modernist poetry by writing nonsense (with no coherent theme, no verse technique, deliberate errors, parody of existing material, free association, and snippets of textbooks) and

---

12. See Insella, ed., *Penguin Anthology of Australian Poetry* and also http://www.ernmalley.com/index.html.

sending them to an Australian journal devoted to modernist poetry in the name of the mythical Ern Malley.

Sixteen poems were submitted, allegedly by Ern's equally mythical sister Ethel as Ern, it was claimed, was recently deceased. These poems were accepted and published, to great acclaim, in a special edition of the magazine devoted entirely to the work of this previously unknown but obviously brilliant poet. Subsequent revelation of the truth of the matter led to the complete humiliation of the editors and publishers, and the ultimate demise of the magazine. Although the publisher subsequently maintained that the poems, although hoaxes, were actually good poetry, it is now hard to read them without finding what previously appeared to be esoteric, mysterious, and in some way meaningful, to be simply hilarious. I particularly like the triumphant ending of "Petit Testament": "And in conclusion: There is a moment when the pelvis explodes like a grenade . . . I have split the infinitive. Beyond is anything."[13] When reading these poems the belief that one is dealing with a literary joke is absolutely essential and, in a similar way the way the parables, and to similar extent other parts of the teaching of Jesus, are understood are transformed *if* one is ready to see humor in them.

Fortunately there are always some who see the real humor in Christ, even though they may be in the minority. Pearson Choate's 1933 novella *The Laughing Christ* is one example.[14] It describes the unexpected reflections of a Londoner called Jones on the implications of seeing various portraits of Christ. The story obviously derives from Choate's own actual experience in the Wallace Art Gallery where he is struck by the contrast between what he considers to be the weak, sentimental, melancholy, and bored-looking representations of Christ of classical art with the more dynamic, humorous, very human (and genuinely famous) portrait known as "The Laughing Cavalier" (1624) by Dutch painter Frans Hals. Choate/Jones wonder whether there should not be some equivalent of "The Laughing Christ." Jones, a painter himself, resolves to fill this gap and the book proceeds to expand on the implications of a view of Christ as one who laughs, compared with all the other representations that there are. In the end Jones decides that the task is beyond him and that it would an idea better written about than painted, a justification for Choate's novella. The central point concerns the way that the notion of a joyful, laughing Christ affects one's understanding of God and, in doing so, it is, as it should be, very much

---

13. Ibid., 195.
14. Choate, *The Laughing Christ.*

a piece of its time, reflecting the implications for the national character in between the wars in England. The conclusions there may not suit the situation elsewhere but the central point is valid: that every age, and every Christian culture and community needs to consider the implications of a joyful, laughing Christ for their own life.

4

Parables, Comic Characters, and the Gospel

Truly I tell you, unless you change and become like little children, you will never enter the kingdom of heaven.

—Jesus of Nazareth[1]

Humor is the royal road to the kingdom of God.

—Donald Capps[2]

In this chapter and the next there is an examination of the various types of humor found in the Gospels and a preliminary categorization of the material.

1. Examples of Jesus' participation in celebrations involving humor
2. Jesus' teaching about responding to his teaching with humor
3. Parable and story
4. Comic characters and situations
5. Images and metaphors
6. Hyperbole and exaggeration
7. Irony and satire

---

1. Matt 18:2.
2. Capps, *A Time to Laugh*, 170.

8. Paradox and reversal

Categorization itself is not the primary objective, and there does not need to be complete exactitude in the distinctions between, for example, irony and satire in every text, nor whether the humor of a specific parable is based on incongruity or paradox. The focus here actually falls on the range of humor and the theological possibilities or purposes involved in it. I will leave to New Testament scholars the examination of the precise differences in humor between the Gospels, and to an assessment of the role of the Gospel writers as editors and humorists vis-à-vis the exact nature of the humor of Jesus himself, though I argue here that the humor as presented is significantly original and fundamentally connected with his character and teaching. He constantly used illustrations, stories, and anecdotes in his teaching, and on many occasions humor was obviously intended. People were meant to be amused or to see the irony or incongruity involved in the situations and characters described. Although one aim was obviously pedagogical, with the various forms of humor intended to lighten and illustrate what being said in order to educate, and sometimes challenge those listening, it is also impossible to think that these illustrations were merely utilitarian adjuncts to his teaching and that they did not arise from a genuine sense of humor.

It may be that the reader does not reckon every single observation, analogy, image, or story listed here to be humorous because humor is very individual and variable, and much depends upon the attitude of the one listening or reading, but the overall picture is of teaching enriched with amusing and ironic observations, sometimes with satirical intent.

Examples of Jesus' participation in events involving humor

Have you ever been to a wedding where you did not laugh? I hope not, for weddings are joyous occasions that deserve great celebration. A wedding without joy and laughter is a travesty, and the absence of laughter would be an indication that something was seriously wrong. If someone does not laugh at a wedding it is probably an indication that they doubt the wisdom of it and fear that it will become a tragedy. It is certainly not normal not to laugh at the celebration of a wedding. Weddings, feasts, and other celebrations feature in the Gospels. The first of the miracles that the Gospel of

John records took place at the wedding at Cana that Jesus attended with his mother and disciples (John 2:1–12). And when it looked like it was fading away as a result of a shortage of wine, Jesus responded to Mary's observation of this by turning a substantial amount of water into wine.

There is no reason to doubt that Jesus laughed at this wedding even though that is not specifically noted here and, anyway, that is of little consequence given that the significance of this wedding is to be found elsewhere, in something more than its normal, human dimension. This is the first of seven miraculous signs recorded in John's gospel and the symbolism of this particular sign is that abundant wine was a sign of the age of fulfilment spoken of by the prophets (Jer 31:12; Joel 3:18; Amos 9:13–14) and it now points to the fact that the kingdom of God was at hand in the person of Jesus. This sign was a revelation of his glory that led to the disciples putting their faith in him (John 2:11). This wedding miracle is more about Christ than the wedding he attended in Cana.

The christological focus is seen in the way that rather than remaining to focus on the wedding at Cana, John's gospel is more interested in moving on to the next two chapters and Christ's own wedding in which he is united with his people. John the Baptist's testimony (in John 3:27–30) about Jesus was that he, John, was merely a friend of the groom, while Jesus was the joyful groom coming to meet his bride.

> To this John replied, "A person can receive only what is given them from heaven. You yourselves can testify that I said, 'I am not the Messiah but am sent ahead of him.' The bride belongs to the bridegroom. The friend who attends the bridegroom waits and listens for him, and is full of joy when he hears the bridegroom's voice. That joy is mine, and it is now complete. He must become greater; I must become less."

Jesus is no longer merely a guest who laughs and enjoys himself at someone else's wedding, he is the groom laughing for joy at the consummation of his relationship with his people. He is the one who laughs above all others.

The wedding theme continues in chapter 4 where Jesus meets the Samaritan woman at Jacob's well. As I have argued elsewhere, John's account of the meeting of the woman of Samaria and Jesus (John 4:1–42) clearly follows an ancient Jewish formulaic pattern of romantic love stories based around meetings at wells.[3] Previous examples include Isaac and Rebekah, Jacob and Rachel, and Moses and Zipporah, and now Jesus comes to meet

---

3. Edgar, *The God Who Plays*, 90–95.

the woman of Samaria and engage in spiritual marriage. John makes the situation obvious by pointing out that the well was none other than Jacob's well, where one of the previous romantic encounters had happened, and by preceding the meeting with an account of John the Baptist telling his disciples that Christ was a groom coming for his bride. He really could not do any more to make it clearer that Jesus is to be understood as a lover seeking his beloved, a bridegroom seeking a bride. The woman of Samaria has had six husbands, none of whom are her real husband, and she is waiting for the perfect seventh. She might not have been beautiful, as Rebekah, Rachel, and Zipporah were, at least not as the world reckons beauty, but in Christ's grace-filled eyes she was indeed beautiful and he became her lover, her true husband, rejoicing and, we can assume, laughing at their union. Something that everyone ought to know about (John 4:29).

The other Gospels make no mention of Jesus' celebration at the wedding in Cana in particular but do make the point that he was well known for enjoying good food, wine, and company. He appears to have enjoyed what we would call wining and dining. How else could the exaggerated accusation of being a glutton and a drunkard have any merit at all? Matthew and Luke record the response Jesus made to the accusation that he was not as ascetic as John the Baptist: "For John the Baptist came neither eating bread nor drinking wine, and you say, 'He has a demon.' The Son of Man came eating and drinking, and you say, 'Here is a glutton and a drunkard, a friend of tax collectors and sinners.'" (Luke 7:34; Matt 11:18) It is inconceivable that one who appreciated wining and dining with all sorts of people, including those known as "tax collectors and sinners," did not engage in great laughter and fun. This connection of Jesus eating and drinking—and laughing—with tax collectors and sinners is not merely evidence of his good nature. It is, as is the feasting at weddings, a theological sign in itself. Both are to be seen as an anticipation, a foretaste of the joy and laughter of the heavenly banquet (Rev 19:6–9).

Jesus' teaching about responding to his teaching with humor

Jesus was aware that there were various reactions to his teaching and he addressed the appropriateness of various responses on a number of occasions. Usually more attention is paid to the dramatically demanding statements (such as "Anyone who loves their father or mother more than me is not worthy of me," Matt 10:37) than to the perhaps somewhat more mysterious references to being like a child as when Jesus said, "I praise you, Father, Lord of heaven and earth, because you have hidden these things from the wise and learned, and revealed them to little children" (Matt 11:25) and "Let the little children come to me, and do not hinder them, for the kingdom of God belongs to such as these. Truly I tell you, anyone who will not receive the kingdom of God like a little child will never enter it." (Luke 18:16) People have persistently resisted the subversive wisdom of Jesus, which not only insists that "the first shall be last" and that "the greatest among you will be the least" but also that adults should learn from children (rather than the more customary state of children learning from adults). Overall, it is hard for adults to learn from children but, ironically, this resistance is evidence of the very need for it because there is much that adults can learn, including learning to laugh like a child.

Children are the finest examples of entering the kingdom of God because their faith is so unconscious, so natural, so much a part of their lives that, unlike adults, they are not encouraged to "have" it, because they cannot possibly be without it! And, unlike adults, they are not warned about losing it because it is so intrinsic to their life and being. Children should not be idealized as though they were chosen because they are good in some sense (they are not always good or completely perfect or righteous), but they do come with completely empty hands and without any of the rationalizations, justifications, explanations, or excuses that are found in adults. As such, children are living illustrations of justification by grace and the best examples of the way into the kingdom of God.

Children are examples to adults in at least two ways. The first is that they possess the humility that comes with being vulnerable and completely dependent upon someone else. The second is the total commitment to life that children express in every facet of their being. Whatever they do, children live and experience life fully in the present, without reserve. They cannot but be committed to life, and to laughter. It is intrinsic to their life and so too an essential aspect of the disciple's joy at redemption.

As well as learning to be like children, Jesus called on those who were his disciples to "be happy." Matthew and Luke record the blessings known widely as the Beatitudes (Matt 5:1–12; Luke 6:20–26). The Greek *makarios*, used for this blessing, was employed by the Greeks to describe the happy state of the gods who lived in peace without trouble, and of the rich who had wealth and no cares. Here it refers to the happy spiritual state of those who share in the blessings of salvation. They rejoice in being comforted, having the kingdom of heaven, inheriting the earth, being filled with righteousness, being shown mercy, seeing God, being called sons of God and having great reward in heaven. This joy becomes laughter and stands in contrast to the unrighteous who laugh now but will soon mourn and weep. Those who follow Christ are to know that they are blessed and that they should "rejoice and be glad because great is your reward in heaven" (Matt 5:12). The teaching of Jesus is clear: joy and laughter ought to be hallmarks of the disciples of Christ.

Parable and story

Telling parables was a well-known form of Jewish teaching (Ps 78:2; Prov 1:6; Ezek 17:2; 20:49; Hos 12:10) that Jesus utilized extensively (Matt 13:3–13, 34; Mark 4:2, 11, 33; Luke 8:10). The following list is illustrative rather than comprehensive. One could certainly debate the existence and extent of humor in some parables but it is not necessary to show that all parables are humorous to make the essential points about Jesus' use of humor. Two parables that contain humor have been discussed so far—the parables of the Unforgiving Servant and the parable of the Banquet, but there are others that contain some dimension of humor.

Hyperbole: Jesus used hyperbole in various ways, not always in parables. Sometimes it can sometimes be difficult to determine when a statement is intended hyperbolically while on other occasions the intention is clearer ("If your right eye (or hand) causes you to stumble then gouge it out [or cut it off]," Matt 5:29–30). As we have already seen the parable of the Unforgiving Servant has the servant owed an impossibly large amount to the king (Matt 18:23–35).

Innuendo: The other parable recounted above, the parable of the Banquet (Luke 14:15–24) contains an implicit reference to the honeymoon period of one of the invitees. Any insistence that this allusion is inappropriate represents the same kind of purtitanicalism that insists that Jesus did not drink wine and that the miracle at the wedding of Cana involved a non-alcoholic beverage. In some social situations it may well appear as a mildly inappropriate reference but such cultural mores should not be applied retrospectively. The enthusiasm of this brand new husband to be with his new bride is very understandable!

Foolish characters: There is a contrast in the parable of the Ten Virgins between five sensible virgins who took spare oil for their lamps when they went to wait for the bridegroom to arrive at his wedding, with five foolish ones who did not. Consequently the foolish virgins are caught short and have to go away to buy more. This mildly unusual situation has its lesson—about the consequences of unpreparedness—emphasized by the even odder, and more amusing, situation whereby the foolish virgins end up being left outside the wedding feast knocking on the door and calling out, trying to get in while those inside are telling them to go away because they do not know who they are! It is not wildly funny but the humor helps make the point. In the parable of the Rich Fool, a rich man plans a life of leisure based on an accumulation of world goods. But he does not control the length of his life and dies without enjoying any of his wealth (Luke 12:16–21). This may only appear amusing to some. It will be a more sober story to others.

Amusing situations: Some parables are very brief: "He also told them this parable: 'Can the blind lead the blind? Will they not both fall into a pit?'" (Matt 15:14, Luke 6:39) This is perhaps so brief that it is easy to miss the humor of the imagery of someone who has a blind guide and ends up in a ditch. Then there is the woman who makes life intolerable for the judge (Luke 18:1–8). Her persistence brings justice in the end. One's opinion as to whether this is funny may well depend on one's opinion of the local judges. If they are lazy or corrupt or poor administrators of time, this may be seen as a satirical observation that raises a nod and a smile. Or perhaps not. Context and perception are important.

Comic or ironic comparisons: As noted above, context is critical in discerning comedy. When stories are told about tax collectors and Pharisees, Samaritans and shrewd officials, one's existing perceptions about their usual character and behavior determines whether one perceives humor or offense or simply a story. The contrast between the Pharisee and the tax collector at prayer does not go well for the Pharisee who would normally be expected to be appropriately devout (Luke 18:9–14). Those who saw truth in the contrast would likely laugh.

The parable of the Good Samaritan is so well known that it can be difficult to view it with a fresh perspective. The contrast between the behavior of the priest and the Levite (religious people with responsibilities to care) and the Samaritan (a much disliked foreigner) would have been surprising to everyone who heard it (Luke 10:25–37). Some would certainly have been offended but anyone with a predisposition against religious officials who did not live up to their responsibilities, or with an appreciation for Samaritans or a dislike of their usual treatment by their Jewish cousins, might well have laughed. And if the parable itself was not humorous they might well have laughed at the offended response of other people!

Derision: It can be difficult to decide when satire becomes derision. The parable of the Pharisee and the tax collector at prayer perhaps belong in this section. The parable of the Tenants certainly does and the Pharisees understood it as a derisive attack on them because their immediate reaction was to look for a way to arrest him, "because they knew he had spoken the parable against them" (Mark 12:1–12; Luke 20:9–19). It pours scorn on the teachers of the law and the chief priests who are likened to thuggish tenants who end up murdering the land-owner's son. This parable is not at all amusing in content; it is only humor in the derogatory sense.

The parable of the Unjust Steward is an intriguing tale of a manager who is about to lose his job. He unjustly reduces some debts owed to his employer in order to ingratiate himself with those who owe the money so that he could later on receive a personal benefit from them. This is nothing other than corruption. But when the master finds out he commends his manager for his shrewdness (though one is not told whether he does anything else about it). The story as a story is not exactly humorous, but it may have raised a wry smile and, despite the owner's recognition of the shrewd behavior of his manager it has to be understood as a critique of such behavior on the basis of Jesus' own interpretation that people like this cannot be trusted with anything ("whoever is dishonest with very little will also be dishonest with much. So if you have not been trustworthy in handling worldly wealth, who will trust you with true riches? And if you have not been trustworthy with someone else's property, who will give you property of your own?" [Luke 16:1–12]). In a general sense the parable is aimed at criticizing anyone who loves money more than integrity and it is only modestly humorous in establishing that point, but the sensibilities of the listener are, once again, important in determining the effect of the parable: "The Pharisees, who loved money, heard all this and were sneering at Jesus. He said to them, 'You are the ones who justify yourselves in the eyes of others, but God knows your hearts. What people value highly is detestable in God's sight.'" (16:14–15) Consequently, precisely because the Pharisees saw this as another direct attack on them it becomes a parable of derision and a cause of laughter in those who dislike Pharisees.

Joyful celebration: A number of parables end very happily with people rejoicing at their good fortune, and just about any story that finishes well has the potential to draw the listeners or readers into that same feeling of joy and happiness. The very simple parable of the hidden treasure is like that (Matt 13:44). The idea of unexpectedly finding treasure in one's field will bring a smile to many faces. Luke 15:1–32 contains three parables in a row that deal with things that are lost. The well-known parable of the Lost Sheep, in which the shepherd leaves the ninety-nine that were safe to seek and find the one that was lost, is followed by the parable of the Lost Coin, in which a woman searches carefully to find a lost silver coin even though she has nine others. Then there is the more extended parable of the Lost Son, in which a son wastes his inheritance in wild living away from home before returning where he is welcomed by his father and becomes the focus of a celebratory feast. His elder brother resents this but is told by his father that it is right to celebrate one who has returned, as it were, from the dead. In all three parables the emphasis is upon the joy that there is at finding that which is lost. The first two parables have exactly the same conclusion: "He [she] calls his [her] friends and neighbors together and says, 'Rejoice with me; I have found my lost sheep [coin].'" There is a universal sense of joy at finding something valuable that has been lost. But the parable of the Lost Son makes the point that if there is such joy and celebration, feasting and laughter in these situations, then there will be more joy in heaven in finding people who have been spiritually lost: "I tell you that in the same way there will be more rejoicing in heaven over one sinner who repents than over ninety-nine righteous persons who do not need to repent" (15:7). True joy in heaven cannot be without laughter any more than the celebrations on earth for the sheep, the coin, and the son that were found could have been without laughter!

The fundamental conclusion has to be that the parables are the most basic evidence of the humor of Jesus. They emerge from a playful understanding of life and they encourage the listener to creatively and whimsically interpret and apply the possibilities inherent in the various situations that are described. They often involve a form of situational humor that is as recognizable as the modern television genre of sitcoms, albeit considerably briefer in form. These parables and their humor are used to teach and to challenge while avoiding more directive approaches. The use of hyperbole, innuendo, foolish characters, comic comparisons, and both derision and joyful celebration accentuate the lightness of the teaching concerning divine action and salvation.

LAUGHTER AND THE GRACE OF GOD
Comical characters and situations

In Jesus' teaching in addition to the often unusual situations described more fully in the parables, Jesus frequently made brief references to people behaving in unusual or irrational ways. The purpose was usually to make a point about some attitude or behavior, such as the way to be generous without reward, the commitment required in discipleship, or the need for humility. While not hugely funny the absurdity of the situation is usually obvious. These comic characters include:

- *the builder who builds without foundations:* the building collapses and, similarly, followers of Christ should lay a good foundation to their discipleship by listening to the words of Jesus (Matt 7:26; Luke 6:46–49).
- *the builder who does not think ahead* and so can't afford to finish the building, which is a reminder that disciples of Christ should consider the long-term cost before beginning their journey (Luke 14:28–30).
- *the king who does not plan his battles* will inevitably lose, and those who do not think ahead about serving Christ had better not become disciples (Luke 14:31).
- *the person who blows their trumpet when they are giving alms* is a hypocrite who has their reward, so don't be like them, instead give without expecting public recognition (Matt 6:2).
- *the two sons asked by their father to work in the vineyard:* one says he will but doesn't, the other says he won't, but does! The point being that it is possible to be surprised: the ones you think will be obedient are not necessarily the ones who actually obey (Matt 21:28–32).
- *the banquet guests who gives themselves places of honor* only end up being humiliated. Humility is better than pride; those who know that they are poor are blessed (Luke 14:8–11).
- *the house owner who knows when a thief is coming* obviously will *not* stay away—going out when you know a thief is coming is foolish! The point is about being ready for when the Son of Man returns (Matt 24:43).
- *the person who puts a lamp under a bed or inside a jar* is obviously foolish. In fact, God's light shines everywhere and everything is known (Luke 8:16). An alternative is that hiding the light will not help

others—your light should shine so that others who come may see it (Luke 11:33).
- *the father who gives his son a snake instead of a fish, or a scorpion instead of an egg* is not a good father. Good fathers, including God, know how to give good gifts to their children (Luke 11:11–13).

Each one of these observations is based on the perception of some incongruity. The imagery is invented and incongruous but it has no point unless it has potential reference to some real situation. Humor is the means by which human activity can be gently corrected.

Most of the comic characters that Jesus refers to are invented but there are two situations where those described in potentially comic terms are real people. One involves mockery and the other a potentially more amusing comic figure.

Mockery and the Pharisees

The Pharisees are described in terms of the kind of scornful humor found in the Old Testament when the Lord laughs at the wicked (Ps 2:4; 37:13). This is certainly a different form of humor but one that needs to be considered. In Matthew the mockery involves the Pharisees being described as making their phylacteries broad and the tassels on their prayer shawls long, so that they will be easily noticed and their attention to prayer and to the law (contained in the leather phylacteries they wore at prayer) would be applauded. This, however, is actually nothing but hypocrisy. The genuineness of their devotion is also questioned by the accompanying observation that they love the places of honor at banquets and being greeted as rabbi in the market place (Matt 23:5–7). Mark has a similarly mocking description concerning their flowing robes and their preference for the important seats in the synagogue and the places of honor at banquets. In this case the ostentation and hypocrisy of the Pharisees is complemented with the accusation that "they devour widows'" houses and, for a show, "make lengthy prayers." Such people, it is noted, will be punished most severely (Mark 12:38–40).

Elsewhere these Pharisees are variously compared to (a) ridiculous people who clean the outside of their cup and dish while leaving the inside dirty (i.e., inside they are "full of greed and self-indulgence," Matt 23:25); (b) whitewashed tombs, "which look beautiful on the outside but on the inside are full of the bones of the dead and everything unclean" (i.e., they are "full of hypocrisy and wickedness," Matt 23:27); and (c) unmarked graves, which people walk over without knowing it (thus becoming unclean themselves, Luke 11:44).

These are strong, stunning charges laid against those responsible for leading the community in religion and morality and they would have angered the Pharisees. There were others, such as the scribes who were similarly offended ("Teacher, when you say these things, you insult us also," Luke 11:45) because they saw the implications of what Jesus said as applying to them as well (most of them were associated with the Pharisees). And what of the others who observed and heard these insults? Well, no doubt some, especially those close to the Pharisees, were extremely shocked and they would not have found this funny in any sense at all. But others might well have laughed, perhaps after getting over their shock, because it is unlikely that there were not others apart from Jesus who also saw the problems of hypocrisy, ostentatious religiosity, corrupt community leadership, and the abuse of widows. There are always more who accurately perceive such things than there those who are prepared to name them as such privately, and even less who are prepared to publicly call them out. But Jesus would not have been alone in his condemnation and there was an audience for his mocking humor.

The abuse to which Jesus referred is not specifically known but it may have involved legalistic decisions contrary to the best interests of the widows or some form of favoritism that discriminated against them, or an unfair manipulation of the tithes and contributions that Pharisees were able to set.[4] Those who saw these injustices might well have found themselves laughing and cheering Jesus on, applauding his courage and feeling encouraged themselves by his plain speaking. In particular, those who had been victims of pharisaic abuse—widows and others—would have rejoiced at this mockery. Some would clearly be empowered by Jesus' words, and being able to laugh at those who claim to have moral power and authority, but who misuse it, is a huge step toward overcoming it. We may not know how many would have rejoiced at this mocking, scoffing attack on bad behavior but some would certainly have laughed and rejoiced at this declaration of justice. The Pharisees were comic characters in the sense that they were the objects of derision.

---

4. Keener, *Bible Background Commentary*, 161.

Peter as a comic character

It is possible that the Apostle Peter was meant to be seen as, amongst other things, a somewhat comic character. In the Gospels and in the Acts of the Apostles he is a prominent disciple of Christ, one of the first called, always first in lists of the apostles, a spokesman of the Twelve, present at the Transfiguration, and usually at the center of any action. He is generally reckoned to be an impulsive character, but was he genuinely comic in personality or perhaps created as a comic character? There seems no doubt that there is comedy in Acts 12, which describes Peter's miraculous escape from prison, though the status of it is debatable: is it simply the straightforward recollection of a single, unintentionally funny event? Or is it the beginning of a comic way of viewing Peter?

Acts 12 begins with genuine tragedy as it recounts Herod's execution of James, the brother of John. This, it is noted, pleased the Jews and so Herod planned the same fate for Peter, who was arrested and placed in prison awaiting a public trial and execution after the Passover. But the church was praying for Peter and on the night before his trial an angel appeared to Peter while he was sleeping, bound with chains between two soldiers. Russell Morton, who sees in the account whole elements of typical Graeco-Roman comedy, thinks the comedy begins with the image of the angel poking Peter with a stick to wake him (12:7) and then guiding him, apparently miraculously, away from the guards and through gates that open themselves![5] It is a surprising story, one that, if it stopped there, would easily please and amuse any early Christian audience as it was told, and probably retold again and again. But there is still more.

Peter now finds himself alone in the street and goes to the house of Mary, the mother of John, where he knew people would be gathering. He knocks on the outer door and a servant girl, Rhoda, comes to answer it. When she recognized Peter she was so overjoyed she ran back inside without opening the door and told everyone, "Peter is at the door!" They proceed to debate this unbelievable piece of news and then consider whether it is Peter or an angel and, meanwhile, Peter is left outside knocking and calling to be let in! Only then do they do the obvious and open the door and find Peter, and at this point the commotion is so great that Peter has to be the one to remind them to be quiet and to allow him to explain.

---

5. Morton, "Acts 12:1–19."

The elements of suspense, surprise, and comedy are then followed by irony as those who were meant to be responsible for putting Peter to death are themselves executed.

In this account one does not have to see any intent by Luke to represent the situation formally in terms of contemporary Graeco-Roman comedy, it was just naturally a story that inevitably would have been repeated again and again in the storytelling style of the day with great emphasis on the humorous dimension.

The mistake at the heart of the story was Rhoda's but it placed Peter in a comic situation and it could have contributed towards the general perception of Peter as a comic character. At decisive moments Peter was undoubtedly one of the leaders of the apostles and while he made mistakes one cannot doubt his outstanding perceptiveness regarding Christ and the gospel of salvation: it was Peter who among the apostles first unequivocally declared Jesus to be the Messiah, the Son of the Living God, and it was Peter who seized the initiative to speak to the crowd on the day of Pentecost in order to interpret to them the death and resurrection of Jesus and the presence of the Holy Spirit, in order to impress on them the need for everyone to immediately repent, be baptized and receive the Spirit (Matt 16:16; Acts 2:1–41). He was a direct and passionate leader, but the uninhibited passion that he had for the gospel also sometimes came across as simple impulsiveness: always asking questions and wanting explanations, trying to walk on water, wanting the best seat, refusing to allow Jesus to wash his feet—and then wanting a complete bath! It was Peter who was seen declaring absolute loyalty and then denying Jesus, falling asleep when he was meant to be on watch, dangerously swinging his sword around, and being outrun on the way to the tomb but going in first without hesitation when they got there. He was, one might say, a large-as-life character. Were his impulsive actions seen as foolish or comedic? Was his personality such that he did not mind, or even enjoyed, laughter at his uninhibited behavior? Had he learned that extroversion could be fun? Did he believe that someone always needs to state the obvious and try the unlikely, and that mistakes could always be forgiven?

Humor with theological intent

Although this survey of humor is not complete it is nonetheless possible to begin to draw together some conclusions. Jesus not only wept, but he laughed and appreciated the humor of life. However, this humor, including the most festive events with which Jesus is connected in the Gospels—feasting with tax collectors and sinners and participating in the wedding at Cana—is not presented merely as evidence of his human nature but rather as a theological sign of the nature of divine salvation. Feasting with tax collectors and sinners involves rejoicing because these are the people who are the focus of salvation, and the wedding at Cana is a sign of future eschatological joy. As a result of this laughter emerges from the joy of those who know that their reward is in heaven and thus ought to be a hallmark of discipleship. In the parables Jesus also utilizes humor with theological intent—using comic situations, characters and comparisons, hyperbole, derision, and joyful celebration to illuminate his teaching about divine action and salvation. Jesus' light-hearted and sometimes comic view of life is closely connected with the joy of salvation.

5

Laughter as the Language of Faith

*I laugh because of a certain, unfailing
confidence in God and his truth.*

—Huldrych Zwingli[1]

Jesus frequently used brief *images and metaphors* in his teaching. Many are simply illustrative and not necessarily amusing. For example, Jesus described himself as the bread of life, the door of the fold, the good shepherd, and the true vine (John 6:35; 10:7, 11; 15:1). These are not intrinsically comical but because they are unusual (a person as a door?) it is possible that some people will perceive them as humorous as well as instructive. Images that are even slightly developed have an increased possibility of humor:

- *"You are the salt of the earth, make sure you don't lose your saltiness"* (Matt 5:13; Luke 14:34–5).
- *"You are the light of the world, let your light shine"* (Matt 5:14).

Other images clearly demonstrate humorous intent—although familiarity with them can make it difficult to see that.

- When giving money, *"don't let your left hand know what your right hand is doing"* (Matt 6:3). What would your left hand do if it did know?
- *"You must become like a child!,"* which, to some, would be a strange and farcical notion; to others an amusing one (Matt 18:3).
- *"You must be born again,"* which certainly mystified Nicodemus who took it too literally (John 3:3).

1. Schmidt-Clausing, *Zwingli*, 12.

- *"Don't give your pearls to pigs."* Not only will they trample on them but they may "turn and tear you to pieces"! (Matt. 7:6). Which is not what one would normally expect.
- *"You can't gather grapes from thorn bushes or figs from thistles"* (Matt 7:16) This can be funny if you start to imagine it happening.
- *"Wedding guests who fast at the wedding"* are ridiculous and behaving inappropriately (there is time for fasting later when the bridegroom is taken away) (Mark 2:19; Luke 5:34).

These are all images of apparently ridiculous situations. They only make sense if one is able to perceive the underlying meaning. Jesus demonstrates a creative mind in forming the images but, more significantly, an astute mind in perceiving the issue that is addressed by the imagery. Those who understand these images actually demonstrate spiritual understanding.

Hyperbole

Hyperbole can be found within parables or separately as part of comic contrasts in individual sayings, as in the following:

- *"Why do you look at the speck in your brother's eye and pay no attention to the plank in your own?"* (Luke 6:41) A visual image used as a criticism of hypocritical behavior.
- *"It is easier for a camel to go through the eye of a needle than for someone who is rich to enter the kingdom of God"* (Matt 19:24; Mark 10:25). A humorous image that acts as a warning to the wealthy.
- *"You blind guides! You strain out a gnat but swallow a camel"* (Matt 23:24). A ridiculous situation used to express criticism of teachers of the law and Pharisees who observe minute aspects of the law while ignoring important matters of justice and mercy.

Exaggeration is useful for making a point. It takes the image into the realm of the absurd and this absurdity transfers across to the underlying point. Criticizing another over some trivial point while doing something far worse oneself is a demonstration of the absurdity of our self-centeredness.

Irony and satire

Irony always emerges from some perceptive insight into a person or a situation. It may be expressed simply as an observation with the implications left to the audience, or it can be directed at a person or group with sarcastic intent. Irony often draws attention to an issue by saying the opposite of what is intended. It is also often a technique where the real meaning and intent is clearer to the audience than to the one to whom the comment is addressed. By its very nature irony can easily be misinterpreted or the meaning debated. Sometimes this ambiguity is intentional.

Do this and live. On one occasion an expert in the law asked Jesus what he must do to inherit eternal life. Jesus asked him what the law said about this and the man replied that it involved love of God with one's entire being and love of neighbor as oneself. Jesus responds by saying, "You have answered correctly, do this and you will live" (Luke 10:25-8). At the time of the Reformation the Latin version of the latter part of this response, *hoc fac, et vives* became a point of great debate: can someone be saved by "doing" the law? Some see this imperative—to obey the law—as being entirely consistent with the fundamental principle of salvation by faith alone rather than by works of obedience, but others, such as Martin Luther, could only see it as being consistent with the principle of grace if it was seen as an ironic statement, something like, "Go on, just try it!"[2]

Use worldly wealth to gain friends. At the end of the parable of the Dishonest Manager Jesus concludes that the people of this world are more shrewd in dealing with their own kind than are the people of light and then he advises his listeners, "I tell you, use worldly wealth to gain friends for yourselves, so that when it is gone, you will be welcomed into eternal dwellings" (Luke 16:9). The lesson here is mixed and somewhat ironic: one should imitate the dishonest manager in one respect (using worldly wealth to gain friends, v. 9a) but then do *completely the opposite* in another (being completely honest, trustworthy, and generous in handling worldly wealth, v.10-3). There is a definite irony in using a dishonest manager as an example for the proper use of money, but it is irony with an unusual twist.

Give to Caesar what is Caesar's. Matthew 22:18-22 and Mark 12:13-7 record the story of some Jews who supported King Herod who tried to trap Jesus into making a politically dangerous statement by asking him whether it was right to pay taxes to Caesar (most Jews paid the tax but

---

2. Screech, *Laughter at the Foot of the Cross*, 55.

revolutionaries objected to any tax at all and some devout Jews objected to images on coins that deified the emperor [although in deference to such sensitivities not all coins in Judea carried that image]). Jesus' reply is, in one sense a statement of the obvious: *the coins belong to Caesar* so let him have them. But in another sense, it is ironic because it challenges the common-sense assumption that *coins belong to the person who has them* and giving them to someone else is a sacrifice or a necessary transaction. This is an observation based on a deeper than usual understanding of the nature of the world and the place of the physical vis-à-vis the spiritual. The statement is thus, in itself astute, ironic, and challenging, and it would also have been downright amusing to those who observed the interaction between Jesus and those attempting to trap him.

Let the dead bury the dead. Various people were becoming disciples and following Jesus but one man said, "First, let me go and bury my father." The general idea is clear but the timing is not. It is unlikely that the father has just died and was awaiting burial (otherwise the would-be disciple would have been with the family in mourning rather than out and about with teachers). It possibly refers to a second burial a year or so after the initial one, when the bones were placed in a special box in a slot in the wall of the tomb. Or it could be a way of delaying things until his aged father actually died. Jesus' response was that the man should follow Jesus and "let the dead bury the dead" (Matt 8:22). Is it funny? Shocking? Ironic? One's understanding of the response depends upon the nature of the request. It seems most likely that it was a Middle-Eastern circumlocution that was aimed at delaying discipleship for some indeterminate time until family responsibilities changed when his father died. If that is so, then the response can be seen as (deliberately?) requiring as much discernment as the request. At one level the answer suggests that what is needed are actually "dead undertakers" (the dead who bury the dead), but at another level (the one that really matters) it is a circumlocution, for those who understand that one should let those who have not found life in serving God and following Jesus (i.e., "the dead") be the ones responsible for the day-to-day responsibilities of caring for the aged and burying "the dead." The implication then is that if this man stays home to take that responsibility that he must be counted among "the dead"! There is some amusement at the first level in the imagery of "the dead burying the dead" and perhaps even more at the second level because the man who has asked for an open-ended deferral of discipleship is being told that this question is, indeed, actually a matter of life and death—*for him!* There is the irony that if he stays home he is joining "the dead who bury the dead."

Paradox and reversal

A number of Jesus' saying involve paradox or reversal. Both feature the use of opposites and they usually involve a degree of surprise for the listener. Paradox involves apparently contradictory conditions which require the listener to think them through carefully to discern the meaning. Reversals involve dramatic changes in situation. The level of humor involved in the imagery and in the concept depends largely on the approach of the one listening.

Whoever wants to save their life will lose it, but whoever loses their life for me and for the gospel will save it. The one who tries to save their (earthly) life by denying Jesus will lose (eternal) life. The one who loses their (earthly) life by declaring their faith will gain (eternal) life (Mark 8: 35). Momentary puzzlement on hearing this paradoxical statement for the first time would soon give way to more serious contemplation if/when the full meaning sinks in.

Blessed are you who weep now, for you will laugh and *Woe to you who laugh now, for you will weep* (Luke 6:21 and 25). There is a double reversal within the one set of blessings and woes. Those disciples who weep now (for whatever reason, it seems) will, in the end, have their sorrow turned into joy and laughter by God (also see Isa 60:20; Jer 31:13; Ps 126:2, and Rev 7:17; 21:4). On the other hand those who are rich and uncaring because they look after themselves and not others (Luke 6:24–5) and who therefore laugh at those who are in need will, in the end, have their laughter turned into weeping and mourning. In this there is both genuine laughter that emerges from joy, and great mourning that is the result of injustice.

The last will be first, and the first will be last (Matt 20:16). This is the conclusion to the parable of the workers in the vineyard who all get paid the same despite starting at different times of the day. Those who complain about this should know that the owner of the vineyard is not being unfair to anyone and is showing grace to those who need to support their families. Those who come last will be treated as those who came first and those who came first will be treated as though they came last. There is humor in this for those who came last and who heard the complaints of those who came first.

A small boy feeds five thousand people. Only John's account of the feeding of the 5,000 includes the information that the five small barley loaves and two fishes that became the basis for the great meal that took place for 5,000 people or more actually came from the lunch of one young boy. Matthew, Mark, and Luke simply have the disciples indicating that this was all they had (Matt 14:13-21; Mark 6:30-44; Luke 9:10-7; John 6:1-15). This could be simply because it was not a very important detail. Or because it somewhat embarrassed them. That, however, is speculation. But John does include the fact and it becomes a fine example of the way that in Christ's hands the smallest contribution can be powerfully used. It is an image of faith that ought to make us smile.

Learning about humor

There is humor in the Gospels but there is no interest in humor for the sake of humor. The humor that is there does not arise from a depository of jokes accumulated for use at appropriate occasions, nor from a desire to just make people feel better. In the Gospels laughter carries more significance than that. As often observed, there is no record of Jesus laughing, an issue which is of concern to some people who wonder what it implies about his character. However, based on (a) a belief in his complete humanity, and (b) the Gospel accounts of his teaching, one can confidently assume that Jesus laughed frequently. Indeed, given the evidence of the parables and all the other observations and allusions described above one can go further and ascribe to him a strong sense of humor. He is man who can be characterized in many ways. He is described as a rabbi, a leader and teacher of disciples, a son and a brother, a friend of tax-collectors and sinners, the Messiah, and many other things as well. He is also, in his teaching and conversation a comic character. He is an astute observer of both common foibles of character and significant incongruities that are injustices. He can produce laughter from observations of everyday life and challenge hypocrisy through irony. To be precise, rather than being one who is presented as laughing he is seen as *the one who causes others to laugh*. Sometimes in joy, at other times in surprise at his uncovering of the real state of affairs, or at the challenge he offers. Sometimes he causes derisive laughter at those who have disobeyed God. He is, in many ways, the laugh-giver. He rejoices and laughs in eschatological joy. Gospel laughter is intrinsically theological in nature.

Little or nothing is said in the Gospels about the casual laughter of everyday life. There are several possible reasons for this. Firstly, there is a cultural issue that the modern Western mind with its automatic approval of the value of laughter needs to consider. In the Graeco-Roman culture of Jesus' day, while laughter was not necessarily negative, the presentation of laughter in written material could impact on the reader's perception of the subject under discussion. Today the modern Western mind tends to assume that normal laughter is socially positive, psychologically healthy, and a sign of good and attractive character. But if it is legitimate for one culture to consider the inclusion of humor to affirm these characteristics then isn't it also appropriate to consider omitting such references in cultures where they might well be misinterpreted?

From Plato onwards there was in classical literature a significant degree of suspicion about humor. Aristotle (Greek philosopher 384–322 BC), Cicero (a Roman politician 106–43 BC), and Quintilian (a Roman rhetorician c. 35–100 AD) all believed that the civilized person ought to be very wary of humor. Nonetheless, the oldest known (certainly not the oldest) joke book comes from the fourth or fifth century BC. Attributed to Philogelos ("The Laughter Lover") with the actual compilers sometimes described as (the otherwise unknown) Hierocles and Philagrios, it is a collection of around 265 jokes, including the following, which probably appeal as much to readers today as to the original audience.

a. A fool who almost drowns swears he will never go back in the water until after he's learned to swim.

b. A man agrees to buy two fifteen-year-old slaves for a friend when he goes to the market and says that if he can't find two fifteen-year-olds he'll get one thirty-year-old.

c. A son in a fight with his father declares that he has always been treated unfairly, "If you hadn't been born I would have inherited grandfather's money!"

d. One of a pair of identical twin brothers dies. When an acquaintance meets the surviving twin he asks, "Did you die, or was it your brother?"

Others seem rather strange today, such as these:

e. A man's child has died and at the burial he remarks, "I'm ashamed to be burying such a small child in the presence of such a large crowd."

f. A centurion addresses the troops: "Today I want you to sit a lot because tomorrow you're going to do a lot of marching."

g. Someone says to a hotheaded senator, "I'd really like to see you when you're free for a moment." The hothead responds, "And I'd like to see you when you're blind and crippled."[3]

Whatever the popular feeling about humor, the general philosophical approach to humor tended to be negative as it indicated lack of self-control and it expressed a feeling of superiority over others. Laughter was certainly appropriate in certain circumstances but not all. The extent to which this cultural attitude influenced the Gospel-writers is difficult to assess as it involves determining a negative—the reason for something not being included. What can be observed, however, which is certainly of significance, is the fact that the Gospels are a very particular genre, one that is focused strongly on the events involving Jesus that lead to salvation: his birth, ministry, suffering, death, and resurrection. In no way are the Gospels biographies, for they leave the major part of Christ's life unexplored. There is very little that is not directly related to salvation and there is a massive focus on the last week of his life. It is not the case that laughter is incompatible with this theology, more that the ordinary laughter of everyday is simply not directly relevant.

The laughter that *is* relevant is that which emerges from theological concerns and it is intimately tied to Jesus' way of seeing and understanding the world and its future. The positive humor that is amusing is not included just for fun, and the negative humor in which he catches out his opponents is not merely a matter of debating tactics or strategy. His humor always relates specifically to the issue at hand and while it may amuse or challenge, it more importantly always reveals something of a spiritual nature about the situation or character. Jesus' humor is not diversionary. The Gospels locate Christ's teaching and his humor in a fundamentally joyful context where laughter is appropriate and always theologically significant.

The Gospels begin and end in joy and laughter. From incarnation to resurrection it is a gospel of joy. Jesus' birth in a stable is reason enough for the angel to declare that this is "good news that will cause great joy for all the people" (Luke 2:10). And it ends with the ascension of Christ which led to "great joy." And the disciples "stayed continually at the temple, praising God" (Luke 24:52–3). Despite the tragedy of the cross the overall context is one of joy, and joy without laughter is not worth the name.

3. Berg, ed., *Philologos*.

The eschatological nature of joy and laughter in the Gospels is seen in the wedding at Cana and the associated discussion of Jesus as not merely a guest at someone else's wedding but as the groom laughing for joy at the consummation of his relationship with his people. He is the one who laughs above all others. Jesus is to be understood as a lover seeking his beloved, a bridegroom seeking a bride. This is also connected with accounts of Jesus eating and drinking—and laughing—with tax collectors and sinners, which is not merely evidence of his good nature but is a sign in itself, an anticipation foretaste of the joy and laughter of the heavenly banquet. Jesus' joy is grounded in his delight in God and in the way that sinners can share in the kingdom of God (Luke 15:7).

Jesus brings joy and laughter to others; his disciples are to rejoice. Those who follow Christ are to know that they are blessed and that they should "rejoice and be glad because great is your reward in heaven" (Matt 5:12). Joy and laughter ought to be hallmarks of the life of disciples of Christ. A sense of humor and laughter are connected with a life of faith. This is not to say that every act of humor or that all laughter is an expression of the Christian life, but those who have faith in God, who believe that there will ultimately be a "unity to all things in heaven and on earth under Christ" (Eph 1:10) will be those who live with a fundamental joy irrespective of present circumstances. And laughter will come from the joy that is within.

Those who have faith will also see the present world very differently. They will share in the humor that Jesus expressed in his teaching. Humor always involves the perception of some incongruity about a person or people, a situation or circumstance or the world as a whole. These are the things that Jesus addresses in the humor listed above. He points them out—sometimes playfully, sometimes ironically, and sometimes in a sharper and more challenging way. But the fact that he is able to find some form of humor—whether light amusement, challenge, or sarcasm—indicates not only astuteness in observation but also a confidence that God will one day resolve all problems. Those who do not have that kind of faith may perceive the incongruity but they will likely find it tragic rather than funny, and will either resort to an optimism that has no foundation or else fall into despair. Humor in the face of the foibles and failures of the world requires faith. Sometimes this humor turns to derision. Those who act unjustly deserve nothing other than to have their injustices pointed out, their characters examined and their actions condemned. Laughter can condemn the wicked, empower the weak, and demonstrate the need for justice.

6

Covenant Laughter and the Comic Vision

*God has brought me laughter,
and everyone who hears about this will laugh with me.*

—Sarah (Gen 21:6)

To suggest that there is laughter and joy in the good news of Jesus Christ is one thing, but it is quite another to find comedy in what is, for some at least, the comic graveyard of the Old Testament. It is not often thought that its serious historical narrative, profound wisdom literature, challenging prophetic exhortation, or majestic psalms of praise naturally lend themselves to comic interpretation. Of course, it is possible to find ways to turn just about anything into humor, but that does not mean that there was humor in the original. Nor do individual flashes of humor alone justify one describing the Old Testament as a great source of humor. Unless, of course, the cultural, linguistic, and historical distance that there is between the formation of the text and today has blinded us to the humor that was intended.

Perhaps the most notable attempt in recent times to promote the notion of a comic vision within the Old Testament is found in William Whedbee's *The Bible and the Comic Vision*, which seeks to overcome the more usual neglect of comedy in order to argue that while biblical tragedy is episodic the comic is a fundamental and ongoing part of the biblical vision of life and faith. Whedbee reviews the evidence for this and notes that the book of Esther, for example, is seen as "the clearest embodiment of the comic vision among all the biblical narratives, representing a brilliantly conceived story in which plot line, characterization of major figures, and rhetorical strategies combine to produce a finely told comedy."[1] It is a story of great reversal in which the villain Haman tries to gain honor for himself while having the Jews exterminated through manipulations involving the king. But in the end the faithful Mordacai receives from the king the honors that Haman mistakenly thought he was to receive himself, and Haman ends up being hanged on the very gallows he built in order to execute Mordecai. It is a an almost perfect plot with a somewhat foolish king, a beautiful, wise, and courageous heroine in Esther, loyal servants and a very wicked villain. Irony abounds and there is definitely a happy—and extremely important—ending, with the Jews, the people of God, being saved from potential extermination. In its original context it is a book that would have been read or heard with great delight.

It is not only the book of Esther that reveals a comic vision of great significance. While Esther is a book of comic reversals, Jonah is a book of comic contrasts that accentuate the nature of divine calling. At the beginning of the story Jonah's response to the divine call to go and preach in Ninevah stands in sharp contrast to the response of other prophets to their call. Jonah does not have the enthusiasm of Isaiah ("Here am I send me . . .") or the obedience of Hosea (who acted immediately) nor even the reluctant acceptance of Moses (who wanted to negotiate terms first).[2] No, instead there is there is simple, blatant disobedience. Jonah is the prophet of the Lord who runs away from God! The point is emphasized by the note that instead of traveling by land to the east, as one would, in order to go to Nineveh Jonah is described as traveling by sea to the west, to go instead to Tarshish. Which is about as opposite as one can get. As he sails away God whips up a great wind and a violent storm but Jonah, by contrast, is so peaceful and comfortable in his rebellion that he sleeps a deep sleep despite the storm. But one cannot sleep when God is creating a storm and he is awoken by the somewhat surprised captain who calls him to do his duty and pray. Overall, Jonah's attitude contrasts badly with that of the crew. Jonah is meant to be a prophet of God, who knows the Lord's will, but here he is becoming a ridiculously obstinate figure while the increasingly fearful crew are trying desperately to save the ship, not only through their seamanship but also by casting lots to try to understand the divine will for their desperate situation. The lot falls on Jonah, and the obvious option at this point is for Jonah not only to concede that he is the cause of their problem but also to change his

---

1. Whedbee, *The Bible and the Comic Vision*, 171.
2. Isa 6:8; Hos 1:3; Exod 3:1—4:17.

approach and to promise to go to Nineveh. But no, perhaps more than a little bizarrely he decides he would rather die than go to Ninevah! And so he volunteers to be thrown overboard instead.

But unlike Jonah the sailors are fearful of God and respectful of life and they continue to do their very best to find safety without throwing Jonah overboard. They try again to get the boat back to land and only when they are completely unable to do so do they finally agree to throw Jonah overboard, and only then with prayer and sacrifice and vows, all of which would have been appropriate actions for Jonah, the prophet of the Lord, if only he had not been so obstinate. It is only through the intervention of a fish that swallows Jonah that his attitude changes and Jonah finally calls out to the Lord, although there is *still* no promise to go to Nineveh. The fish then spews him out onto dry land and, in a sense, the story starts again, with God calling on Jonah to go to preach in Nineveh. Jonah's disobedience to the first call (in 1:1—2:10) is now contrasted with his obedient response to the second call (3:1—4:11). This does not, however, resolve the situation or bring the contrasts to an end. Jonah will go and preach in Nineveh but, unlike the gracious and compassionate God, he does not have his heart in his preaching and he does not actually want the people of Nineveh to be saved. Once again Jonah declares he would rather die than see that happen. What is wrong with him!?

So when he gets to Nineveh, which is described as a vast city, he marches in to one place and gives what is characterized in the text as a very short and blunt message (simply "Forty more days and Nineveh will be destroyed," 3:4) and then leaves. But it is no good for Jonah; his reluctant preaching actually has dramatic effects! Everyone in Nineveh is convicted, lives are changed, they all call on the Lord and are saved. Now these are the very results that every preacher dreams of, but Jonah is miserable at his success and instead of being glad at it he becomes very angry. At this point a vine appears that grows to provide Jonah with shade. But it is really there to be an object lesson in grace and when it dies the next day God points out that it was inappropriate for Jonah to have more concern for the vine than for the people of Nineveh. The story ends with a question that challenges the reader or listener to consider their own attitude.

Throughout the story God is not only shown to be gracious and compassionate but also very much in control despite the antics of those called to be his messengers. Each time Jonah resisted God something unusual occurred in the natural world. Jonah fled from God and a great storm blew up. He still refused to go to Nineveh and asked to be thrown overboard and a fish swallowed him. He preached without wanting a result and a vine was used to teach him a lesson. Jonah may be rebellious but God controls the whole world and is compassionate and deeply concerned about those whom others, even his messengers, despise. This is a story in which the theological message comes through an arresting and somewhat comic plot with an anti-hero who is, paradoxically, greatly used by God.

Genesis as humor: from Adam to Joseph

Whedbee interprets other books and passages in the light of a gracious, comic vision that rejoices and laughs at the actions of God in the world, and Whedbee is even prepared to consider as part of this vision those books that, for one reason or another, are *least* likely to be perceived as comic in any way, such as the book of Job with its focus on suffering and the erotic love song of the Song of Solomon. But it is Genesis that is the focus of Whedbee's attention. He sees it as having not just comic episodes but a comic vision throughout and he makes the bold claim that it is the "dominant generative source of comedy in Western literature."[3] The present task, however, is more modest than that of assessing the comedic implications of Genesis for Western society. I aim simply to evaluate whether Genesis was intended to present the account of God's dealings with the world with any sort of comic dimension.

The early part of Genesis (chapters 1–11) begins, of course, with a narrative which moves from a vivid description of the creation of the world to a focus upon the creation of humanity and then the disobedience of Adam and Eve and the consequences that emerge from it, which seem to work their way into the story of Cain and the murder of Abel, the flood in the time of Noah, the covenant, and the events involved in the tower of Babel. In laying out this account of God's relationship with the world Genesis provides its readers with reason to enjoy the whole story, not only joyful events such as the account of divine creation, but even the more sobering report of the sinfulness of humanity. The story is full of paradox and incongruity and through these it makes its theological points. There is the contrast between divine creator and human creature with their interaction expressed anthropomorphically and often with dry humor. God is described as strolling in the garden in the cool of the day, as any ancient Near Eastern gentleman might. The story

---

3. Whedbee, *The Bible and the Comic Vision*, 15.

contains, in the Hebrew, a number of puns (adam from soil; eve who gives life; woman from man; and the nakedness of Adam and Eve compared with the shrewdness of the serpent). There are some unusual reversals of social norms (as when Adam leaves his parental household to join with Eve), some humorous characterizations (evil that is in the form of a serpent; the man who blames his wife; the wife who blames the serpent; and the serpent—dare one say it—who doesn't have a leg to stand on; as well as the God who asks, "Where are you?"). As the story progresses God continues to be presented anthropomorphically (God is "sorry" for making humanity and he shuts the door on Noah in the ark; Noah—the "righteous man, blameless in his generation"—is found to be drunk and naked; and the story of the tower of Babel has people who believe that they can build a tower that will reach the heavens being investigated by a God who comes down to take a close look at it (Gen 6:6, 6:9, 7:16, 9:21, 11:1–6). The significance of these divine-human encounters is not diminished by imagery and events that are presented in very ordinary, human, and potentially humorous ways.

The latter part of Genesis (chapters 37–50) is taken up with the story of Joseph. The dramatic and comedic potential has notably been expressed in Andrew Lloyd Webber and Tim Rice's enduring pop cantata, *Joseph and the Amazing Technicolor Dreamcoat*. While there is no doubt that some of the comedy is created specifically for the musical, its success is based on the fact that the original story itself has a comedic dimension. It is a story full of drama and tragedy and amazing circumstances. There are characters who are larger than life and one gets a sense of the dramatic thrust at the very beginning with the light-hearted account of Joseph's apparently egocentric dreams about greatness (his brothers' sheaves of wheat bowing down to his own; and no less than the sun, moon, and stars bowing down to him) which he relates not once, and not twice, but three times to his father and brothers, despite their obviously annoyed responses clearly indicating that they did not take kindly to the suggestion that he would rule over them and the rest of the world. (One has to ask, what kind of person does that three times?) The story proceeds with drama (such as the abandonment of Joseph by his brothers) and the risible (the attempted seduction of Joseph). The comedy in the story fulfills various functions as it can be used to provide a gentle critique of character (thoughtless Joseph who aggravates his family is seen as amusing), to celebrate the divine serendipitousness of life (a rejected and enslaved dreamer becomes a powerful leader), and as a way of dealing with tragedy (to balance and to put into perspective the drama of rejection and imprisonment).

Does this kind of exploration and analysis of the text and the cultural basis of humor result in sufficient evidence to conclude that there is a thoroughgoing comedic vision within the Old Testament? The careful, detailed, literary analysis done by Whedbee and others that shows the presence of more humor than might otherwise have been thought present is cumulatively impressive (despite having to overcome the scholarly version of the inevitable problem of trying to explain humor).

Nonetheless, humor is not found everywhere. There are passages that are decidedly grim and they are many people who do not see the Old Testament as a barrel of laughs. If reckoned on a proportional basis one probably would not determine the Old Testament to be very comical. But volume alone is not a good measure of theological significance. One has to ask about the theological purpose that humor might have within Scripture and consider what, if anything, that Scripture itself says about the hermeneutics of humor. One possibility, of course, is that humor is purely *incidental* to the fundamental message. That it is simply designed to lighten difficult teaching and to brighten tragic narratives. Thus one perceives humor as a part of the biblical writers' communication technique whereby the humor is an adjunct to the frequently theologically challenging account of God's dealing with his people. In this case the humor is external to, and not a part of, soteriology. It is thus akin to pulpit humor that aims to regain people's attention when it has faded, and to enliven otherwise overly serious reflections. On the other hand, a very different possibility is that humor is actually an *intrinsically* and theologically significant part of the story and thus included for more significant theological reasons rather than out of pedagogical or literary motives. In this case the humor is central and not incidental and, therefore, it does not have to prove itself to be ubiquitous in order to justify the perception of a theologically comic vision within the Old Testament.

This latter possibility emerges from within the central part of Genesis (chapters 12–36) where there is an explicit connection of theology with laughter. The account of Abraham and Sarah and the Lord's declaration of a covenant with their descendants and the eventual birth of Isaac is a key story where laughter is very much in focus and of great significance. It begins with Abraham's skeptical laughter at God's declaration that he and Sarah will have a child. He is too old for that! Later, Sarah laughs as well, but then wants to deny that she did, and then, when it all comes about, she laughs joyfully rather than skeptically. In the end it is God who is laughing. This account is the hermeneutical key, connecting covenant purposes with laughter and the comic vision of life.

Isaac and laughter as faith in the covenant

This narrative begins with God promising childless Abraham that he would be the father of "a great nation" (Gen 12:2). But it seems that this is not going to be possible for no child is born for some time and so God reiterates the promise and faithful Abraham believes and God credits this to him as righteousness (Gen 12:2; 15:5; 15:6; 17:4). But there is still no child and after a time Sarah sees it as her responsibility to give her servant Hagar to Abraham so he can have a child with her. Ishmael is duly born, but the relationship between Sarah and Hagar becomes difficult. God once again reiterates the promise of children for Abraham. This promise, it must be understood, is not *just one more gracious act of God* to enrich the lives of his servants. It is not just one more promise among many that God makes and keeps. No, the promise of a child is *a sign and a proof of the promise that God would create a people, a nation, with which he would enter into a sacred covenant*. Without the child there could be no nation and no covenant. The promise is central.

Now God is very specific that Sarah will have a son and Abraham, in response, laughs, albeit, apparently, to himself (Gen 17:17). This was a laugh of skepticism, of doubt in the promise of God. But this is not merely the promise of a personal miracle, it is nothing less than a promise that God would bring blessing and salvation to the world. And Abraham laughs at it! But in response a gracious God simply reiterates the covenant—yet again! And more time passes. Then God tells Abraham one more time, through one of the three somewhat mysterious visitors at Mamre (closely connected with the presence of "the LORD") that Sarah will have a son. And Sarah, listening from outside overhears and, like Abraham, laughs at the possibility (18:10-2). The chance of bearing a child seems so small. This too is a laugh of doubt, of incredulity. But when Sarah laughs, she is not knowingly laughing at God, but at what some guests in her husband's tent have said. Now God questions Abraham, "Why did Sarah laugh?" This is not necessarily a rebuke but Sarah begins to be worried—was this laughing at God? And so she lies, "I did not laugh." But she had, and it was exactly what Abraham had done, and Abraham, moreover, knew exactly with whom he was dealing.

Theologically, the skeptical laughter of both Abraham and Sarah represents doubt about the promises of God concerning his forthcoming covenant with the people of Israel. It represents a human and skeptical response to God's offer of grace. But God does not punish the unbelief or doubt of either Abraham or Sarah. Indeed, God does not appear to be offended, but simply goes ahead with what has been promised and thus shows their laughter to be wrong. Sarah becomes pregnant and a child is born who is named Isaac, which means "he laughs." And in the end Sarah can say "God has brought me laughter and everyone who hears about this will laugh with me" (21:6). There is a shift in the story from doubtful laughter to joyful laughter.

Sarah's words that others will laugh with her mean more than simply that other people will be pleased and amused by her story of childlessness, doubt, and then immense joy. They are an unconscious prophetic indication that in this very birth God's covenant promise is being fulfilled and that others can, along with Abraham, Sarah, and Isaac, participate in it and rejoice. In this birth a nation is being created, the people of God is being formed, the promised covenant that will ultimately embrace the world is happening. Sarah surely does not fully understand the prophetic dimension of this fulfillment of God's covenant promise but there is this deeper level that those who laugh with Abraham and Sarah are not merely entertained by an amusing story, but they are receiving the blessing of God's covenant. This joyful laughter is nothing other than the result of God's covenant, symbolized in the name of the child who was the firstborn of this new community of God. In this story the meaning of laughter is changed and deepened. Unbelief and skeptical laughter have been replaced with joyful, believing laughter and joy. Those who participate in the covenant will be those who laugh for joy. Those who laugh for joy at God's covenant are the faithful.

The laughter motif continues throughout the life of Isaac. After his birth his elder half-brother, Ishmael does something in regard to Isaac that Sarah saw and which displeased her (21:9). The interpretation of the text is a matter of some controversy but it seems to involve a pun on Isaac's name ("he laughs"). It could be that Ishmael was laughing at the baby Isaac, or mocking him in some way, or playing with him in some way that Sarah found offensive. The lack of clarity concerning what it was that Sarah saw has led to speculation about whether it was simply laughter or mocking or whether it involved some form of abuse. But if laughter in the story of Isaac is seen in a theological light the precise nature of the problem that Sarah had may well have been left obscure because it is fundamentally irrelevant. Just as the laughter of those who hear Sarah's story of the birth of Isaac is not meant only as an indication of its entertainment value, but rather as a sign of the deeper possibility of others participating in the covenant, so in this situation the problem that leads to Sarah driving Hagar and Ishmael away is merely the occasion for God's new dealing with Hagar and the promise of a great nation through Ishmael (21:18).

This theological interpretation means that Isaac is, in a serious sense, a comic character in that he is the one who was born to prove the divine promise that all will one day be able to laugh with Sarah at the grace of God. He is a central character in this comic vision and his name declares his role. Isaac has become the focus of joy and laughter because of the circumstances surrounding his birth at such a late age for Sarah and Abraham and his name is not a comment on his looks or his ability to joke but a theological statement about the covenant that was created through his birth.

There is no need for Isaac to be telling jokes to be a comic character. Indeed he is comic in a different sense, and yet it seems possible that the story of his life does actually intentionally continue laughing at and with Isaac. At the very least, as one considers the life of Isaac, one has to wonder whether much of what could be merely innocuous detail might not actually be intended to show that even a comic character can be greatly used by God. Consider the story of his marriage: when Isaac was a young man Abraham sent a servant to find him a wife. One might ask why Isaac did not go himself. Is he not competent for a task that is of such personal importance? Is Isaac likely to make a mess of it? Or perhaps Abraham just wants him to be at home with him? Anyway, the servant goes and the narrative describes how the servant wonders, at length no doubt, about how to be certain that he is making the best choice, given that it is such an important decision. So he decides that the ideal way to find a wife for Isaac is to ask a woman he meets by chance at a well to give him some water and if she gives him water and helps water his camels, that she will be the one, the perfect match for Isaac. Now, one might see this as an act of complete faith in God. Or, given the fact that in ancient Near Eastern times the obligations of hospitality to travelers and of women to men meant that there was virtually a guarantee that he would get a positive response from *any* woman at the well, one might see it as a much less than ingenious way of finding

God's choice for Isaac. Kaminsky says that it is like saying, "I'll take the first woman who understands basic hospitality."[4] In any event, Rebekah becomes the chosen one.

Isaac, Rebekah, Abimelech, and Esau

The story then moves on to the circumstances of the first meeting between Rebekah and Isaac and this can be characterized in very different ways. The NIV says that one evening Isaac "went out into the field to meditate" and while doing so, saw a number of travelers approaching. From the vantage point of her camel Rebekah simply sees a man in the field and so she dismounts and asks a servant, "Who is that man?" On finding that this man is, amazingly, the very man she is coming to marry she takes her veil and politely covers her face. All very civilized. However, an alternate reading of this is that one evening Isaac went out into the field to urinate or defecate,[5] where he was inadvertently seen by Rebekah, who was less than impressed and she "falls off her camel" (which is a more literal rendering of the text than the NIV's "she got down from her camel" and the NRSV's "slipped quickly"). She then asks a servant who the man is and is less than impressed to find that he is none other than her future husband (ta da!), at which point she veils herself out of embarrassment at the way things were going. Now Isaac's poor timing might be seen as inadvertent, but things like this seem to happen to some people more than others. They certainly happen to Isaac, which may say something about his character. Indeed, virtually all of Isaac's dealings with Rebekah, Abraham, Esau, and Abimilech that are recounted in the narrative show him as a somewhat awkward and less than socially adept individual. He does not come across as clever or resourceful. Kaminsky describes him as a typical schlemiel (an awkward or unlucky person).[6]

Isaac thinks that he needs to be smart when meeting the powerful Abimelech but he actually engages in what turns out to be a quite unnecessary deception. He portrays Rebekah as his sister rather than as his wife

---

4. Kaminsky, "Humor and the Theology of Hope," 363.

5. This meaning is only a possibility. It relates to a possible reading that he was "digging a hole" but other suggestions include planting something, taking a walk, conversing with friends, gathering wood, enjoying the breeze, or praying, complaining, or lamenting to God. Vall, "What Was Isaac Doing in the Field?"

6. Kaminsky, "Humor and the Theology of Hope," 364.

(Gen 26:6-11). This is a deceit that on the one hand has (a) the potential to protect Isaac from being killed if Abimelech decides that he wants the beautiful Rebekah as his own, but which also has the effect of (b) leaving Rebekah at *greater* risk than if she was described as Isaac's wife and (c) *rendering Isaac completely impotent* (because Isaac is, in this situation, now unable to even attempt to protect his wife and is only able to protest that Abimelech should leave his sister alone). Isaac is something of a bumbler and he does not come across as a protective patriarch let alone as a clever diplomat or a potential hero.

When Isaac is older and apparently under the impression that he is soon to die he decides to give his final blessing to his eldest son, Esau (Gen 27:1-30). As it turns out, however, he misjudges his timing and (happily) does not die for another twenty years (Gen 31:38 and 35:29). Nonetheless, the blessing is to be given and so Isaac sends Esau off to hunt for game and to prepare him a meal prior to being blessed. Jacob, however, schemes to receive the blessing himself by impersonating Esau and his success in this is mainly due to Isaac's obtuseness rather than Jacob's skill. It is noted in the story that Jacob's charade is open to being discovered for what it is at a number of points. Isaac observes that Jacob returns too quickly with game, and he notes that the voice belongs to Jacob and not to Isaac, but he does not suspect anything. He imagines that Jacob's (alleged) hunting clothes smell of the fields even though they were actually Esau's best clothes freshly turned out from being stored in Rebekah's house and he is fooled by the goatskin which he mistakes for human hair. Whether because of his character (is he gullible?) or his age he is fooled by Jacob.

Subsequently, Esau seems to inherit his father's lack of astuteness. Despite the family history of avoiding wives from among the Canaanites Esau married two Hittite women who, not surprisingly, "were a source of grief to Isaac and Rebekah" (28:6-9; 26:34-5). Later, when Isaac sends Jacob to find a wife from within Uncle Laban's family, Esau finally realizes how displeasing his marriages were to Isaac. Moreover, he comes (mistakenly) to believe that this is what lies behind Isaac's blessing of Jacob. So in a confused attempt to rectify the situation he goes and marries a non-Canaanite woman, Mahalath, who was Ishmael's daughter. But although he is now marrying within the family his choice is, again, faulty, because by marrying into Ishmael's line he is merely guaranteeing that his descendants will not be a part of the covenantal lineage.

Laughter and the covenant

What does all this mean? The story of Isaac is certainly not laugh-a-minute humor, but rather, at one level, a relatively gentle characterization of social awkwardness and fumbling within the family. The original readers and listeners, especially those in the family line would have been very much attuned to the nuances, the implications, the mistakes, and the humor involved. But the overall narrative is, of course, primarily an account of God's action in creating a covenant people and of his relationship with them and, at another level, laughter plays an important role as an expression of faith. The humor, the characterizations, and the frequently ironical development of the narrative is not present simply to entertain or to keep one's attention or for any other purpose that is not intrinsic to the narrative itself. The purpose is theological and it focuses on the role of laughter in responding to God's grace in the covenant. The central feature is the birth of Jacob and the laughter of Sarah and Abraham. Much of the humor is only discerned if one reads the text with the right attitude. It is frequently ironical and paradoxical, sometimes tragic, but always joyful in the end. God does not lose control and divine purposes are pursued in such a way that they bring joy and laughter. This laughter is faith in God and a participation in divine joy.

7

God, Heaven, and Humor

If you're not allowed to laugh in heaven, I don't want to go there.
—Martin Luther[1]

If God does have a sense of humor, what is it that God finds funny? And what does God's sense of humor imply concerning the divine character? In dealing with this one has to, inevitably, deal with the issue that concerns some people—that theological humor is controversial, not only because all humor is, to some extent, potentially controversial but because religious humor often appears to be more sacrilegious than sacred. Of course, the perceived degree of controversy with any humor, let alone religious humor, varies significantly from one individual to another and according to context. When you stumble and fall I might laugh, but I don't when it happens to me. And when your grandmother falls over it is upsetting, but when that pompous old git who thinks he knows everything slips then it can be humorous. Unless he really hurts himself. The humor of the situation also varies according to the level of social sensitivity about the subject, often increasing, for example, when it involves sex, politics, or religion. In short, religious humor and any consideration of God's sense of humor can be controversial.

There is, however, Christian humor that is generally considered to be relatively harmless. Church newsletters and pew-sheets often have cartoons about Gospel stories such as Jesus walking on the water (with cartoons speculating about what baby Jesus did at bath time) or his everyday interactions with the disciples (Jesus playing poker with his friends saying, "Lazarus, I'll

---

1. Manser, comp., *Westminster*, 225.

raise you.") Or even novel interpretations of the resurrection (a somewhat frustrated Jesus showing his ID to doubting Thomas). Some depictions have a more political edge with Jesus, for example, as a refugee "of Middle-Eastern appearance" being denied entry to the country. At this point the humor takes on a more serious purpose. Indeed, it sometimes become more than a little pedagogical, such as the apocryphal situation attributed to Theresa of Avila who, while in a hurry fell off her donkey into the mud. "Lord", she allegedly said, "Why would you let this happen? It couldn't have happened at a worse time." And the response that she heard was, "This is the way I treat all my friends." To which she boldly replies, "Well, no wonder you have so few of them!" In so doing she simultaneously,

a. demonstrates a positive attitude to adversity
b. expresses confidence in her relationship with God
c. attributes a sense of humor to God, and
d. suggests the possibility of having a playful relationship with God.

Equally well-known is the Jewish joke repeated in various forms in numerous situations (including the introductory monologue to the musical *Fiddler on the Roof*) in which the dreadful disasters that have befallen the Jewish people are recounted alongside the conviction that this is part and parcel of being the chosen people of God. Consequently, the plea is, "Next time, God, please choose someone else!" In these there is a level of ambivalence (a key aspect of humor) concerning who, exactly, is the butt of the joke, whether it is the people involved or God. Is it appropriate to laugh at God? Or perhaps at a *caricature* of God? And if it is a caricature (of an old man in a beard?) then is it then actually God at which one is laughing? And, by the way, does God find those jokes amusing? The creators of the Monty Python film *The Life of Brian*, a film reckoned by some to be blasphemous, argued that they were not making fun at Jesus but at Brian, a character born on the same day, and in the stable next to Jesus, who repeats some of what Jesus said and was consequently confused with him and who thus becomes the unintentional leader of a movement. But is that claim a joke in itself?

On other occasions the connection between religion and humor is truly controversial. Contemporary debate about this began with the satirical, so-called "Danish cartoons" published by the newspaper *Jyllands-Posten* in 2005. There were a dozen cartoons that depicted the Islamic prophet Mohammed (or, in one case a Danish schoolboy named Mohammed) sometimes in unflattering ways. As far as the newspaper was concerned it was a statement about the tendency towards self-censorship concerning criticism of Islam that they saw emerging in other publications and in public debate and the cartoons involved a legitimate criticism of Islam. For others, especially some Muslim people, they were problematic not only because of their view that it is blasphemous to visually depict Mohammed, but also because the cartoons involved what they saw as false and offensive depictions of his character and actions. The subsequent debate pitted strong convictions about free speech against concerns about social unrest. The controversy was linked with all sorts of other political and religious grievances that led to both peaceful protests and dangerous riots resulting in hundreds of deaths. Islam, of course, is theologically different to Christianity, not least in the fact that, due to the incarnation itself, depictions of God and Christ are not considered intrinsically offensive. But specific representations can still be offensive even though one would hope that it would be less likely to involve the same level of violent response from Christians if Jesus were subject to this kind of cartoonish criticism.

Questions concerning the *morality* and the *legality* of public comment, whether humorous, artistic, academic, scientific, or political are not identical, but moral judgments are frequently expressed in legal forms. Some countries have laws about offensive or hate speech or the vilification of racial or religious groups but they vary considerably, either defending the right of expression or making certain forms of speech illegal in an attempt to reflect the moral views of that community. For some the Danish cartoons and other potentially offensive publications ought to be exempt from judgment precisely because they are humorous or, more generally, artistic, in nature rather than political or social. This moral exemption for humor and art, and sometimes for specifically academic and scientific presentations, is sometimes reflected in the law although there is, obviously, plenty of scope for vigorous debate about whether artistic or humorous intent in general, or unspecific cases, ought to be exempt.

The moral status of humor is thus a much contested issue. It is possible to consider five possibilities in which humor is seen as,

a. *morally inappropriate* (that is, generally problematic and spiritually detrimental, even if occasionally acceptable),

b. *morally variable* (with value judgements dependent on the intent and the context of specific situations),

c. *morally neutral* (that is, amoral or exempt from moral judgment as an activity without a moral dimension),

d. *a moral good for the present age* (a positive human virtue, albeit one that can potentially be abused),

e. *an eternal good* (that is, a dimension of the age to come, and a divine attribute).

It is certainly no secret that the present argument in this chapter is that none of the first four options are as theologically satisfying as the final one.

The problem of humor

By the third century the early church had developed the view that laughter was intrinsically problematic. The prevailing view was that laughter was to be limited and treated with great caution because it was dangerous to one's spiritual life. Consequently, there was particular opposition to laughter among those most committed to seeking spiritual perfection, that is, among those within the earliest monastic movements. The Essenes imposed a penance of thirty days on those who laughed foolishly, the rule of Pachomius forbade joking and, according to the teaching of Ephraim the Syrian, "Laughter is the beginning of the destruction of the soul."[2] From the perspective of our later era it is possible to see that this opposition to laughter derived from a particular form of biblical interpretation (in which injunctions against coarse humor were generalized) combined with asceticism (which denied the value of physical desires), rationalism (which was opposed to the incongruities and absurdity of humor), and platonic dualism (separating the perfect spiritual life from earthly pursuits) as well, of course, as the inevitable influence of a solitary lifestyle that is not itself conducive to laughter. At the time these influences led to three principal justifications that were given for humor being seen as spiritually dangerous: it was argued that humor was unspiritual, unethical, and untruthful. The situation today is, of course, very different to that because in Western culture humor itself is not generally seen to possess those negative connotations that previously existed. Indeed, it is more commonly perceived to be an intrinsic good. Yet an examination of the ancient problems still has value

---

2. Morreall, "Philosophy and Religion," 216.

for today because humor is still neglected and treated as suspect, often for many of the same reasons as in the ancient church.

The first problem for many in the early and medieval church was that humor was intrinsically *unspiritual* in that it exhibited a lack of those characteristics then considered essential for the spiritual person: moderation, humility, and self-control. For Clement of Alexandria (c. 150–215 AD) speech was the fruit of the mind and so humor, which is typically ridiculous or absurd, was an indication of a mind that was in need of control. Some humor was acceptable ("when given vent to in the right manner it indicates orderliness") but it had to be kept in check in case it showed an unfortunate lack of restraint. It was accepted that the human person was "a laughing animal" but such laughter was to be subject to careful discipline for it could easily be the case of slipping into scandal.[3] The Fathers lauded the Greek philosophers emphasis on self-control. Basil (c. 330–379 AD) wrote that "raucous laughter and uncontrollable shaking of the body are not indications of a well-regulated soul, or of personal, dignity, or of self-mastery."[4] As we saw earlier, *The Rule of St. Benedict*, which became the standard set of monastic rules for Western monasticism, has a chapter on humility that sets out a ladder of twelve steps that lead to true humility. The tenth step is that the monk is not given to ready laughter for "only a fool raises his voice in laughter" (Sirach 21:23) and the eleventh step is that a monk speaks gently, seriously, quietly, briefly, reasonably, modestly, and without laughter.[5]

A second problem with laughter was that humor could be *unethical*. Laughter and humor were connected with the desires and the delights of the physical body and thus with the sins of the body including lust and anger. The biblical injunction for the faithful to avoid "obscenity, foolish talk or coarse joking" (Eph 5:4) was often interpreted as an indictment on all humor. The commitment of the early ascetics to avoiding anything approaching sin meant that many good and normal parts of life were avoided in case they inadvertently gave rise to sinful desires. Consequently, laughter did not have to be seen as intrinsically sinful to be avoided, it was simply a dangerous pleasure that had the potential to lead people away from righteousness. John Chrysostom (c. 347–407 AD) warned people about the dangers of any delight or pleasure because of the possibility that "somewhere in the depth of the pleasure some iniquity should lie

---

3. Clement of Alexandria, *Paedogogus*, Book II Chapter V.
4. Morreall, "Philosophy and Religion," 216.
5. Benedict, *Rule*, 61 and 162.

enveloped" and so one should "search closely, and if thou discoverest it, hasten away!" The disciple of Christ should therefore not only avoid those things that are sinful but also those things that are indifferent, that is, not sin in themselves, but which are "yet apt to make us stumble against sin. For example; to laugh, to speak jocosely, does not seem an acknowledged sin, but it leads to acknowledged sin." Some versions of his teaching includes further advice that makes the situation very clear: "Avoid not merely foul words, and foul deeds, or blows, and wounds, and murders, but unseasonable laughter itself, and the very language of raillery; since these things have proved the root of subsequent evils. Therefore Paul saith. 'Let no foolish talking nor jesting proceed out of thy mouth'. For although this seems to be a small thing in itself, it becomes, however, the cause of much mischief to us."[6] In this ascetic version of the spiritual life even that which is good can become a source of evil.

Humor was also problematic because it was seen as being *untruthful* in that it conflicted with the dictates of reason and descriptions of reality. Humor inevitably involves incongruity, irrationality, caricature, or some other distortion of either logic or the actual situation being described and if taken literally, without an awareness of humorous intent, then it will be taken as inaccurate, crude, or offensive. Human laughter, like that of both Abram and Sarah in their reaction to God's gracious promise of children and many descendants (Gen 17:17; 18:10-2), is simply doubt and skepticism rather than faith. Humor was particularly problematic for those who saw the spiritual life as being advanced through rational means and by a constant awareness of the vagaries and sins of the present world. This was expressed by Basil in his "On the Perfection of Solitaries," such that even if laughter was not aggressive or obscene that it was always irrational and never serious—and these were seen as fatal flaws. The Christian, he said, "ought not to speak evil, to do violence . . . He ought not to indulge in jesting; he ought not to laugh nor even to suffer laugh-makers."[7] An intense focus on the spiritual dissolution of the present world leaves little room for humor when describing it. Augustine of Hippo, for example, disapproves of laughter in his sermon on Psalm 126 ("our mouths were filled with laughter") observing that when a baby is born it is able to cry but is not able to laugh, and the righteous person is the same because the spiritual truth is that as long as the

---

6. Chrysostom, "Homilies," XV, 7 and 11.
7. Basil, "On the Perfection of Solitaries," Letter 22.

believer is in the physical body then they are actually exiles from the Lord, and an exile cannot think of home without tears.

This form of dualism—which conceded that moderate laughter was possibly (though rarely and only moderately) appropriate to everyday life but inappropriate to anyone seeking spiritual perfection, inevitably diminished the fundamental value of laughter. And while it was the dominant view when asceticism was the preeminent form of spiritual life it is a view that has not completely vanished in more libertarian times. In his plea for serious (i.e., non-humorous) preaching in a comedic culture David Murray argues that laughter is appropriate in everyday life but not in preaching and the process of spiritual growth and learning. The two, it is argued, are not compatible because the preaching of the Lord Jesus, such as the Sermon on the Mount, was not humorous, the principal spiritual subject is serious (as it involves judgment and potential damnation), and the world is full of pain and sorrow. Thus it is important to avoid the superficiality of humor.[8] This critique of non-serious preaching and humorous spirituality is helpful in some ways but it ultimately fails, because (a) it does not recognize that the Lord's teaching was more light-hearted and humorous than Murray assumes, (b) when discussing salvation there ought to be less focus on the fear of damnation than on the joy of salvation, and (c) the world not only has suffering and tragedy but is also blessed and full of grace and humor. Yet his critique reminds us that when humor fails it can mean more than a joke being missed. Humor can, indeed, be a weapon wielded with dangerous intent. This is a point worthy of exploration and a contemporary assessment of the misuse of humor might well include the following five sins of humor: it can be aggressive, derogatory, excluding, obscene, and superficial.

The morality of humor

Humor often involves making fun of someone and this can happen at various levels of intensity extending from gentle mockery and friendly teasing through to sarcasm and even outright aggression involving open ridicule and other cruel forms of humor. This can be disturbing to people and for most there comes a point where the humor starts to evaporate, although that point is significantly influenced by whether one believes that the mockery is deserved or not. Sometimes it certainly is, as when God mocks the wicked who oppress the poor, the needy, and the righteous, and those who

---

8. Murray, "Serious Preaching."

oppose God's people with lies and violence. God laughs at them because God knows that "their day is coming" (Ps 37:12–5).

The fact that humor frequently involves making fun of someone has given rise to a superiority theory of humor that argues that humor (either as a whole or in part according to different theorists) derives from a feeling of superiority in which one laughs at other people's misfortunes, their foolishness or their mistakes, their attitudes or behaviors. This idea extends back to Plato, who held that people laugh at others' misfortunes and Aristotle, who said that humor was made of those people and things that were mistakes or deformities or worse than the average.[9] Much later Thomas Hobbes (1588–1679) became a champion of the idea that humor arises from a sudden awareness of some superiority or advantage in one's own situation by comparison with that of others.[10]

Superiority theory is not, however, in itself, a full explanation of the essential nature of humor, although it does make it clear that humor has purposes that extend beyond mere entertainment. Humor can be used to condemn inappropriate and unjust actions and thus it can be used positively to make serious and profound moral, social, and political statements. It can also be a means of making make inappropriate, unfair, cruel, excluding, or aggressive comments, While the most egregious examples of aggressive humor are easily perceived as such, other expressions of humor are more difficult to assess because of the ambiguity that is part and parcel of the humor. This ambiguity creates uncertainty about the real intent of it and the way the point of the humor is perceived. The humor is confronting but whether it is *intended* positively as a means of revealing injustice or negatively as an attempt to denigrate people can be difficult to discern and so the perceived *effect* of the humor can vary significantly. Consequently, the moral status of the humor is difficult to establish and it is well understood that some people use humor for precisely that reason, that it masks the intent and creates a plausible justification for what would otherwise be seen as an unjustified attack. A joke reckoned by some to be simply harmless humor that is predicated on human differences can be perceived by others as racist or sexist and the problem is that humor is ambiguous by nature; it is always playing with incongruity and what may be humorous to one sets the ground for discrimination, contempt, aggression, and exclusion against another.

---

9. Plato, *Philebus*, 45–49 and Aristotle, *Rhetoric and Poetics*, 229.
10. Hobbes, "Human Nature," 46.

One way to avoid this moral ambiguity is to argue that humor is, by definition, morally neutral and thus exempt from moral judgment. The amoralist view holds that humor functions within the realm of imagination and is essentially anarchic and specifically focused on that which is incongruous, inappropriate, and out of place. But, it is argued, the presuppositions and the attitudes necessary for the humor to function need not be ones actually held by those involved. These attitudes and ideas only function within the imaginary world of humor. As Conolly and Haydar argue, "when we joke we only entertain ideas and do not actually hold them."[11] The common expression of this is found in the "it's just a joke" defense against claims of offense.

The element of truth in this defense of the amoral position, that humor frequently involves suppositions that need not be actually held by those involved, needs to be acknowledged. But this does not mean that there is no moral dimension to the humor. Even when there is no intent to offend or exclude it has to be recognized that humor has social effects, sometimes subtle and ambiguous, that have to be taken into account. The effects of humor do not live only in the creative, abstract world of humor. Sexist humor, for example, can decrease the perception of the seriousness of rape among men and can lead to the objectification of women. These kind of effects have to be taken into account in any moral reckoning.

However, if one argues that humor is not an abstract, morally neutral activity, but rather an activity with moral implications for the real world then it would seem that any participation in the humor, that is, an appreciation, rather than a rejection, of it, would be a form of moral commitment. This implies that anyone who finds a genuinely offensive sexist or racist joke to be funny, even for a brief moment, is guilty of being an active participant in a morally objectionable activity. Instinctive laughter at such a joke is taken as an indication of one's attitude towards the issue at hand and the claim "it's just a joke" would fall on deaf and disapproving ears. De Sousa, for example, argues that the claim that in humor one supposes various attitudes without actually holding them fails because "emotional attitudes are unlike beliefs in that they cannot be hypothetically adopted"; therefore, "insofar as the attitudes endorsed are evil, so is the laughter itself."[12] On this view, those who have found humor in jokes that express views or activities that they actually believe to be racist or sexist

---

11. Conolly and Haydar, "The Good, the Bad and the Funny," 122 and 131.
12. De Sousa, *The Rationality of Emotion*, 276.

or problematic in some other way ought to confess their sin. If, however, one accepts that humor is a complex, multi-layered phenomenon then it may well be appropriate recognize that witty and humorous elements can coexist with the offensive within the one piece of humor. Generally speaking there is no doubt that there can be more than one theme or idea in a humorous situation and even offensive concepts can be communicated in clever and striking ways. Finding a humorous dimension in an offensive joke does not necessarily mean that one is participating in the morally offensive act. An instinctive response that finds humor in a joke that, on reflection, demonstrates offense does not necessarily make that person complicit in any moral hurt that is taking place. It is important, however, for there to be a more considered assessment of the humor that takes into account any offense involved and this will inevitably result in the sense of humor being diminished. Such an assessment should involve the kind of principles found in the following two biblical injunctions.

The first is to focus on that which is *good*, as the Apostle Paul said, "whatever is true, whatever is noble, whatever is right, whatever is pure, whatever is lovely, whatever is admirable—if anything is excellent or praiseworthy—think about such things" (Phil. 4:8). The second is to do that which is truly *helpful* to the other person especially when there are different perceptions regarding the nature of the humor involved. It is possible to engage in robust and challenging humor for good reason, but it can be misinterpreted and so care must be taken. In response to a question about whether it was appropriate, when a guest in someone's house, for Christian believers to eat meat that had previously been offered to pagan gods Paul argued that it was appropriate because, after all, the gods are actually nothing at all (1 Cor 8:1–13). What he then said about eating meat in a situation where there are different perceptions can easily be applied to what one says humorously, "Be careful, however, that the exercise of your rights does not become a stumbling block to the weak. For if someone with a weak conscience perceives you engaging in apparently inappropriate humor won't that person be emboldened to do the same? . . . if what I say causes my brother or sister to fall into sin, I will never speak that way again so that I will not cause them to fall."

The humanity of humor

Most moral problems associated with humor revolve around the obvious ones of obscenity, the giving of offense, and its use as a means of aggression. But even when humor is apparently inoffensive it can be problematic, as the early Fathers pointed out, if it is either excessive or superficial. Some might not consider superficiality a specifically moral issue but for the ancient fathers too much entertainment and too little seriousness was fundamentally untruthful in that these things drew constant attention to that which was unimportant and presented a distorted and inaccurate picture of the nature of the world. Excessive and superficial humor did not represent the fundamentally spiritual nature of the world. The church fathers were focused upon seeing all things in a spiritual light and so while it was possible for humor to have its place in the present world, because it had little or no spiritual value it was to be strictly regulated and downplayed. The way to eternity in an ascetic age is through suffering, sacrifice, and denial rather than through laughter.

Consequently, it might be assumed that there is little that is positive to learn about laughter from those who so firmly reject it, but that would be to see only half of the picture. The Fathers failed to see the place of laughter in the spiritual life but they were absolutely right to focus intently upon those things that do contribute to spiritual growth and eternal life. Their problem was the fundamental dualism with which they functioned, which meant that laughter could only be a good of any kind within earthly life. If one removes that dualism then joy and laughter can become important components of a life that is directed towards eternity and laughter can be more than a good for the present age and as *an eternal good,* a dimension of the age to come. This goes further than the more modern view of humor which, unlike the Fathers, sees it as a temporal good, though only for the present age. Kierkegaard—that philosophical but also melancholy Dane ("the melancholy," he suggested, have the best sense of the comic"[13]) argued that humor enables one to comprehend the major dimensions of life in all its breadth and ambiguity and is made possible by the same features that make a religious life possible. Thus humor is a reflection of, and stepping-stone towards the ultimate leap of faith and may be seen as the highest form of philosophy, but it is neither faith itself nor the best form of life possible. Humor definitely belongs to the temporal even though it is to

---

13. Quoted in Amir, *Humor and the Good Life,* 181.

be understood as part of the second-best form of life, one that is essential in attaining to the very best. He said that he could not live without humor and he considered Christianity the most humorous of all religions. He claimed that when he was young he had a dream in which he was caught up into the seventh heaven where all the gods sat in assembly and, surprisingly, they gave to Kierkegaard the privilege of making a wish. "Will you," asked Mercury, "choose youth, or beauty, or power, or long life, or the most beautiful maiden, or some other glorious thing?" When Kierkegaard responded he asked for one thing only, "That I may always have the laugh on my side." At first the gods said nothing, but then they burst out laughing. Kierkegaard reports that in his dream he thus assumed that his wish was to be granted, and, he comments, "I found that the gods knew how to express themselves with good taste."[14]

Kierkegaard became the most formative influence in overcoming the traditional bias against humor and promoting it as having a positive role, albeit one limited to the temporal realm. Kierkegaard's influence is, however, closely connected with more general trends associated with the development of the modern notion of humor. These include the secular process of internalization and individuation and the development of the modern sense of the self as a private, interiorized being. This cultural shift in the understanding of the person as related to both humor and Christ is illustrated by two influential dramatic presentations of "the man" Jesus Christ, one in the USA and the other in England.

In 1925 Bruce Barton published *The Man Nobody Knows* in which he carefully avoided the existing stereotypes of Christ as an earnest, somber, mild, or even weak and somewhat melancholy person in favor of a more rugged, entrepreneurial characterization of Christ as a very earthy, practical leader with a sense of humor, a jokester who was amused by such things as turning water into wine. The book was wildly successful, a bestseller, and yet it was also subject to significant criticism from those who felt it was a distortion of the person of Christ and an apologetic for modern entrepreneurial business practice. Nonetheless, it brought into the public arena a conception of Christ as one who, among other things, had a strong sense of humor. The new and somewhat surprising notion that Christ had a sense of humor was also present in Dorothy L. Sayers's very different but perhaps even more controversial and influential presentation of *The Man Born To Be King*, a series of twelve radio plays written in contemporary

---

14. Cited in Donnelly, "Divine Folly," 392.

language and broadcast in 1941 to 1942. The character notes provided by Sayers describe John the Baptist as a strong, authoritative figure, but with "no sense of humor" and a one-track mind. Jesus, on the other hand, is a complete contrast to John. His authority is innate and not acquired and he has a robust sense of humor.[15]

It was, more specifically though, Kierkegaard who set the direction for twentieth-century writers such as Reinhold Niebuhr who wrote positively and theologically about humor. Although Neibuhr's neo-orthodoxy involved a deep understanding of human sinfulness, the world as a place of evil, and the problems involved in being a person of faith, he nonetheless found a real place for humor in the life of faith. Humor and faith, he argued, both deal with the incongruities of our existence and both are expressions of the freedom of the human spirit. But he is well-known for his assertion that humor is a prelude to faith, and not a substitute for it. One comment of his is often quoted: "Laughter must be heard in the outer courts of religion; and the echoes of it should resound in the sanctuary; but there is no laughter in the holy of holies. There laughter is swallowed up in prayer and humor is fulfilled by faith."[16] This has been interpreted in two ways. The first, and more usual interpretation, suggests that the exclusion of laughter from "the holy of holies" is absolute and a recognition of the fact that humor is a temporal good rather than an eternal one. Some judge that this is only right and proper, while others see it as a concession to the older conventions concerning the limitations of humor and a failure by Niebuhr to follow through where his argument was leading. The second interpretation suggests that Niebuhr did follow through with his overall argument and the point is not that humor is excluded or rendered unnecessary by faith, but rather that humor is "fulfilled by faith."[17] It is only the *deficiencies* of humor that are to be seen as excluded from the holy of holies and its true nature is included in the holy of holies by virtue of the fact that it is to be found fully *within faith*.

The holiness of humor

Perhaps Niebuhr's own argument was sufficient to take humor into the holy of holies but he did not, explicitly at least, get to that point and it seems he

---

15. Sayers, *The Man Born to be King*, 86.
16. Niebuhr, *Discerning the Signs*, 111–12.
17. See the contrast between Hyers, *And God Created Laughter*, and, Capps, *A Time to Laugh*, 436.

followed traditional theological precedent when he left humor outside. Even though he considered humor to be a temporal good and a precursor to faith, rather than the outright moral problem that it had previously been, this did not lead him to see humor as an eternal good. Although the prevailing opinion was against humor it was, nonetheless, a contested issue and this debate about laughter in heaven can be seen in two well-known sayings, one from a specialist in laughter and the other a specialist in theology. The specialist in laughter is Mark Twain, speaking through a quotation on Pudd'nhead Wilson's *New Calendar*, to the effect that "There is no humor in heaven." The contrary opinion is attributed to the theologian and Reformer Martin Luther who declares of heaven that "if there's no laughter I don't want to go there." If it were possible an actual debate about laughter between Mark Twain and Martin Luther would certainly draw a crowd!

Twain's view came about because as a humorist he well understood the dependency of humor on pathos. The foundation of everyday humor lies in the incongruities, injustices, and agonies of life and this may be seen, with varying degrees of sophistication in anything from the unintended effects of a misplaced banana peel to the grim humor of those at war. On the other hand, when everything is perfect there is no incongruity, nothing out of place, no pain, no sorrow, and no humor. This is why Pudd'nhead Wilson's calendar notes, "Everything human is pathetic. The secret source of humor itself is not joy but sorrow. There is no humor in heaven." [18] The calendar could also have quoted Kierkegaard who said, "The comic belongs only to the temporal because all contradictions are canceled in eternity."[19]

Twain's argument, or at least the view he allows to be expressed in the calendar quotation, is actually one part of a broader theological argument that there is no laughter in heaven. The first part argues this on the basis of *the perfection of eternity*, while the second part does so on the basis of *the passionlessness of God*. They are closely connected arguments. The second part, which Twain does not directly deal with, argues against humor in heaven on the basis that God is "passionless" and thus has no sense of humor. The notion of a *passionless* God is, in classical theology, itself derived from the *immutability* of God. The divine attribute of immutability is, it is argued, necessary in order to preserve the notion that God cannot be acted upon, cannot be affected by others, cannot be controlled or changed by people or any other part of creation. The implication of this fundamental

18. Twain, *Following The Equator*, 119.
19. Quoted in Amir, *Humor*, 181.

assertion of the sovereignty of God, as expressed, for example, in Thomas Aquinas,[20] is that if God is truly sovereign and thus immutable and unchanging then God is necessarily *eternal* because being immutable means there can be no sense of "before" or "after" with God, who remains the same "yesterday, today, and tomorrow." God is thus timeless or eternal and therefore also without passions that necessarily involve change over time. This is a view of God expressed in the Westminster Confession of Faith, which describes God as the one and only "living, and true God, who is infinite in being and perfection, a most pure spirit, invisible, without body, parts or passions; immutable, immense, eternal, incomprehensible." The result of this is that without passions or changes it is not possible to have humor. This part of the argument leads on to the issue dealt with more directly by Pudd'nhead Wilson's calendar, to the effect that this divine changeless perfection is reflected in the life of the ultimate kingdom of God which does away with everything that is changeable, especially those things that are tragic distortions of God's true intention.

Luther's approach operates very differently and argues that commonsense thinking dictates that life without laughter is not worth living. Ask yourself whether you would want to live in a world where there were no jokes, laughs, grins, smiles, or witticisms, where nothing was funny or even mildly amusing, and the whole of life was unrelentingly serious and unfunny. Many would reckon that this would, indeed, make life unbearable. However, thinking this does not make it so, as has been shown, that there are philosophical issues that are raised by the notion of divine perfection as applied to the world and to the nature of God that need to be answered.

If one begins with a monotheistic understanding of the nature of God then the argument that begins with divine immutability has force. The unchanging constancy of God obviously protects the other attributes of God, such as divine goodness and justice, from arbitrary change: God is therefore *always* good and loving and merciful. But, as has also been shown, this makes it difficult to entertain the idea of a God with passions such as love and humor. Polytheism, in contrast to monotheism, has no problem with humor. The gods laugh continually because they have, by definition, different natures, attitudes, and behaviors and these can lead to different opinions and conflicting thoughts and action. Consequently, the gods, precisely because they are conceived as being different, can be amused, and amusing, and argumentative as well. These qualities however, are the very ones that

---

20. Aquinas, *Summa Theologica*, Pt.1, Qn.9, Art. 1.

lead to the inevitable collapse of polytheism as a system of thought and belief. Being able to live, in a polytheistic system, in accordance with the moral qualities of whichever god one chooses may initially sound more attractive than having to live, in a monotheistic system, according to the moral qualities of the one and only God, but in the end this kind of ultimately self-serving approach inevitably degenerates. And it is not only the followers of the gods who have problems, the relationships between the gods tend to conflict and collapse. Interestingly, although it might usually be reckoned that it is the potential for conflict between the gods that leads to their demise, Nietzsche says that it is actually laughter that does it. He tells a story about the way the gods laughed themselves to death. One day, Nietzsche said, a grim, bearded, jealous god declared to the other gods, "There is only one God. Thou shalt have no other Gods before me!," at which the other gods slapped their knees and fell about, and died laughing! Leaving only one—rather jealous—God alive.[21]

Polytheism has laughter but tends to disintegrate while monotheism has an internal strength and moral consistency which makes laughter problematic. But, theologically speaking, Christians, of course, are not so much monotheists as they are trinitarian. The conviction that there is one God has to be seen in relation to the conviction that there is a genuinely essential three-ness about God that transforms the whole structure of theological thought and makes it clear that God is relational in a unique way. Nor is trinitarian thought merely a sub-species of monotheism, it is its own category of thought, and not one primarily predicated on abstract philosophical logic but on the historical fact of the incarnation. In this very particular way God is revealed as the relational, passionate, dying God who is loving Father, incarnate Son, and everlasting Spirit. In philosophical terms this means being co-equal, co-eternal, and with an immutability that has to be seen as a constancy of nature that includes, rather than excludes, the desire to be a passionate, loving, and gracious God who is essentially, through incarnation, involved with the temporal, the human, and the changeable. The relational statement that "God is love" (1 John 4:8) is the biblical equivalent to the philosophical notion that God is three-in-one. A strictly monotheistic God might exhibit or even "become'" love—when a world is created that God might love—but only a God who is more than monotheistic, who is a three-in-one relationship, can "be" love eternally and essentially. Eternal love is the love of Father for the Son and the Son for the Spirit and all for

21. Nietzsche, *Zarathustra*, third part, ch. 52.

each other. This eternal love pre-exists creation but then overflows in love for the creation. And it is a love that gives rise to great joy and laughter, not only within God but in creation as well.

The humor of heaven

There is a close correlation between human and divine humor despite the fact that human humor is reliant on some incongruity, irrationality, or inequity, things that are said not to exist in God's eternal kingdom. But the claim that "all contradictions are canceled in eternity" should really be that "all *temporal* contradictions are canceled in eternity." There is an even more fundamental incongruity or "foolishness" of the gospel, that is of the incarnation and the work of Christ, that is "wiser than human wisdom" (1 Cor 1:25). Here is an incongruity that is intrinsic to the divine, a God who became a man, transcendence and immanence together, a king who becomes a servant, a God who is uncreated and yet born, a God who dies! There is expansive room for divine laughter here!

There is great laughter in salvation because of the wonderful incongruity in that God has done what a righteous judge should not do (Prov 17:15; Isa 5:23) and declared the guilty to be innocent! The imprisoned are set free and evil is overcome. The gospel is nothing other than laughter and joy at knowing both the nature of God and the work of salvation, and human humor, although greatly joyous, is but a poor analogy of it. Christians ought to rejoice much more than they typically do. It is good to follow the example of the children of Israel who learnt about the law of God from Ezra: "And all the people went their way to eat, and to drink, and to send portions, and to make great mirth, because they had understood the words that were declared unto them" (Neh 8:12, KJV).

There is a divine sense of humor that is based on incongruity and paradox that is consistent with the essential nature of God because it involves the incarnation and salvation. This humor is not just an "add-on" feature, or a human projection that is unconnected with the inner nature of God. It has often been wryly noted that "God created humanity in God's own image and humanity has returned the favor ever since," pointing toward the human tendency to interpret—and distort—the nature of God by using purely human concepts. But the passion, the love, the joy, and the laughter of God are not the result of transference from human nature, they are attributes of God.

The attributes of God are sometimes categorized by systematicians who like order and who want to clarify the understanding of God. This can be done in various ways and they are inevitably both useful and problematic. In some taxonomies certain attributes are described as "essential" or "incommunicable" (those attributes that are unique to God such as the aseity [self-createdness] and the infinity of God), while others are "communicable" or "relational" (which have some analogy in human nature, such as love, goodness, and mercy). This distinction raises the issue of the comparability of the relationship between human and divine natures. Although the one word—*nature*—can be used of both the divine and the human this ought not, as Friedrich Schleiermacher pointed out, be taken as implying that they are two instances of the same category, "For how can divine and human be thus brought together under any single conception, as if they could both be more exact determinations, coordinated to each other, of one and the same universal?"[22] The two do not really belong together in that way. The divine is not, for example, simply, an expanded, enhanced form of human nature. The problem is that human language labors with an impossible task of describing the divine in human terminology. The only justification for even attempting this is the fact of the incarnation—that God has first revealed divinity in human form. The sense in which humanity shares attributes with God has to be qualified in this way. Human and divine love, for example, are both correlated to each other and yet are distinct. So is human humor connected with divine humor in that it is founded on rejoicing in the incongruous and the paradoxical, but so too are they distinct in regard to the incongruities and paradoxes that they rejoice in. Those that form the basis for temporal humor are resolved in the life and work of Christ which, paradoxically and joyfully, is the new foundation for eternal humor.

Divine laughter is not a projection from human nature; indeed, the reverse is true. Human humor is a function of the process of deification by which God transforms humanity into God's own likeness. This is a process begun in creation with humanity being made "in the image of God" (Gen 1:27) with the ability to be joyful and laugh in faith, and completed in redemption with humanity finally and fully being conformed to the image of God and able to rejoice and laugh, not merely with, but *at* God and what God has done.

The Apostle Paul speaks of this divine plan to transform humanity when he says, "For those God foreknew he also predestined to be conformed

---

22. Schleiermacher, *The Christian Faith*, 392.

to the image of his Son" and when he encourages believers to "put on the new self, which is being renewed in knowledge in the image of its Creator" (Rom 8:29; Col 1:9-10; Eph 4:22-24). This process of becoming like Christ is put perhaps most strikingly in 2 Peter 1:3-4, which speaks of God's "very great and precious promises" which enable humanity to "participate in the divine nature." This likeness to, or union with, God produces great joy and laughter at the greatest of all paradoxes, and the greatest incongruity, the humanization of God and the deification of humanity! This paradox was expressed by Athanasius as "He was made man that we might be made God."[23] This "participation in the divine nature" (or theosis, deification, or union with God) is not a divinization that makes humanity equal to, or the same as God, but at the same time it is much more than sharing together in a coalition. It is not merely being part of a community, and it is closer than a relationship with a spouse or counselor. The imagery points towards a much more intimate and organic union, as seen in the language of "sharing in one body" and "being part of one vine" (1 Cor 12:12-27; John 15:1-8). There is no human equivalent to the spiritual union that is involved in being "in Christ" and having "Christ in us." It is simply not possible for one person to be "in" another human person in the way that believers share in relationship with Christ. Believers are "hid in Christ" (Col 3:3-4), a spiritual union for which there is no perfect analogy. The one whose "spirit rejoices in God my Savior" (Luke 1:47) knows and experiences the will, the purposes, and the nature of God in a new way (John 14:26; 15:15), is not anxious about tomorrow (Matt. 6:34) and anticipates the final coming of Christ with joy and laughter. This is what Karl Rahner calls "redeeming laughter,"[24] which is essentially the deepest praise of God.

Humor always means seeing something differently and surprising oneself and others with a new perspective. It may mean seeing the absurdity of evil and injustice or, more significantly, the paradox of the incarnation, the incongruity of God made man or the glorious absurdity of humanity deified. These are especially worthy of laughter! The humorist is aware of the incommensurable, the paradoxical, and particularly of the failure of the sternly ethical attempt to work one's way to God, something which is most worthy of being laughed at! The humorist knows that laughter is the way to come to God and is "the closest thing to the grace of God." Laughter is spontaneous evidence of personal faith and trust in God; it is the primary

23. Athanasius, *On the Incarnation*, 84.
24. Rahner, *The Content of Faith*, 150.

expression of joy in the Lord, and the closest, most intimate and instinctive articulation of an experience of God.

The involuntary nature of laughter truly reveals the underlying attitude. As a young Christian I sometimes wondered, as perhaps many do, about the honesty of my own faith and commitment. Human nature has so many layers of intentions and motives that it is easy to doubt one's own convictions. But I soon realized that there are some things that cannot be doubted because they cannot be faked, since they operate at a deeper, more instinctive level. These include being emotionally moved when others are saved or blessed and one vicariously shares in their experience; spontaneously rejoicing in times of worship; and breaking out in joy and laughter on hearing of the wonderful, amazing work of God. This kind of laughter is nothing other than an expression of one's participation in the life of God.

8

Grace and Truth through Laughter

Laughter is the closest thing to the grace of God.
—Attributed to Karl Barth

Humor has been examined from every possible perspective, thus producing, amongst others, psychological, physiological, philosophical, and sociological theories. Yet no one has provided a truly satisfying, overarching scientific or philosophical theory that has achieved complete consensus among humor theorists. Considering the matter historically there have been three dominant explanations, with the most ancient based in the philosophical claim that humor is grounded in feelings of *superiority*, as when we laugh at someone's foolishness. It focuses on issues relating to relative power and control. The second, *relief* theory, is more physiological or psychological in nature and thus a more modern theory attuned as it is to the development of these sciences. It argues that humor is the expression of emotional or nervous relief that occurs as a potentially difficult or dangerous situation is resolved well. Here the focus is on emotion and relief. The third, and now the most widely accepted theory, is that all humor is based in the observation of some *incongruity*.

The question for this chapter is whether any of these explanations relate to theological considerations of laughter. A theological theory of humor—or a theological theory of any other human or natural phenomenon—is not an alternative to scientific explanations of a physiological, psychological, or sociological kind, but an explanation of a different order. It provides a reason for humor that is more related to Aristotle's final cause, which seeks to explain ultimate purposes rather than the material, formal, and efficient causes that answer questions about the processes involved in the various forms of physical and logical causation. Nonetheless, a theological explanation needs to be consistent with any valid scientific explanation. And for those who accept the theological perspective, the correlation may also confirm the appropriateness of a particular theory and it may even make a contribution towards a deeper scientific understanding of the phenomenon. It is certainly possible and often beneficial for there to be interaction between the different levels of causation within an overarching theory.

As far as a complete theory of humor goes, it is accepted, on the one hand, that incongruity theory deserves a preferred status, while, on the other hand, it is to be reckoned as being incomplete because it does not finally provide an explanation as to *why* incongruity is actually humorous, and why sometimes it is not. This very rational theory of the essential irrationality of humor needs another level of development, one that, it is argued here, can integrate scientific and theological dimensions of humor, and this can best happen through an examination of the role of play. Play has psychological and sociological purposes that relate to humor. However, play and humor also have very important spiritual and theological roles that relate to ultimate, eschatological purposes. The theological and spiritual aspects of play can correlate with scientific and philosophical theories of human playfulness and humor, with incongruity having an important role. The incongruous nature of humor has, in fact, in the past been connected with play in the work of a number of humor theorists, but this connection has not been widely accepted (although the noted play theorist John Morreall has taken this approach).[1] The aim here is to outline a little further the superiority, relief, and incongruity theories and then to incorporate theological and spiritual dimensions into a play theory of humor that incorporates the important role of incongruity.

Superiority theory

The oldest philosophical discussion of laughter is found in the *Philebus*, one of the later dialogues of Plato dealing with he saw as the best form of life.[2] He considers questions about who or what is to be laughed at, and why that should be the case. Laughter, he suggests, occurs when there is an underlying anxiety about the possible superiority of another person, and is an expression of the satisfaction that occurs when some event or observa-

1. Morreall, *Philosophy of Humor*.
2. Plato, *Philebus*.

tion reveals that they are actually more foolish, not so able, or are lesser in some way. This is the foundation of what has generally become known as the superiority theory of laughter, although Plato's various comments do not really constitute a complete theory. This view of laughter as involving comparative superiority-inferiority sees laughter primarily as ridicule and has an aggressive edge to it, as well as an element of ethical judgment because the one who laughs has, or at least believes that he or she has, the moral high ground. Other forms of laughter exist in Plato's thought but they are not so important in defining the essence of laughter, because they are more the result of emotions which override rationality and self-control, which have high value for Plato.

In general terms Aristotle followed the same line, believing that laughter was based on feelings of superiority concerning that which was considered ugly, deformed, mistaken, or below average. But in contrast to Plato he was prepared to see a more positive dimension to other forms of laughter, which he saw as useful for relaxation and refreshment. He noted the comedic value of the unexpected and hinted at the role of incongruity in humor. There was, he felt, an appropriate level of laughter that fell between the extremes of humorlessness and buffoonery.[3] He remained reserved about the morality of humorists like satirists and writers of comedy, who he considered to be evil people.

These observations about laughter originating in a sense of superiority benefited from being a part of what became the philosophical foundation of Western thought and they were largely taken as given, even though they had to wait until the time of Thomas Hobbes (1588–1679) for them to be put into a theoretical framework. In his essay "Human Nature," Hobbes gave a psychological account of the person and their passions in which he defended the view that laughter is based on a comparative judgement of our own superiority: "I may therefore conclude that the passion of laughter is nothing else but a sudden glory arising from sudden conception of some eminency in ourselves, by comparison with the infirmities of others, all with our own formerly."[4] Hobbes also accepted that there were other aspects of laughter but they were secondary, he insisted that in laughter one *really* is dealing with jealousy, self-interest, and ridicule at the weakness of others. This continued the influence of the superiority theory among European philosophers with the German Georg W. F. Hegel (1770–1831) call-

---

3. Aristotle, *Nichomachean Ethics*, IV.4.
4. Hobbes, "Human Nature," 46.

ing laughter "an expression of self-satisfied shrewdness";[5] the Englishman William Hazlitt (1788–1830) asserting that "we laugh at absurdity . . . at deformity . . . at mischief . . . at what we do not believe . . . to show our satisfaction with ourselves, or our contempt for those about us, or to conceal our envy or our ignorance";[6] the Scot Alexander Bain (1818–1903) arguing that laughter was occasioned in "everything where a man can achieve a stroke of superiority, in surpassing or discomfiting a rival";[7] and the Frenchman Henri Bergson (1859–1941), noting that "it is the trifling faults of our fellow-men that make us laugh."[8] In more recent times this view has adapted to evolutionary theory with Anthony M. Ludovici arguing that "all laughter is the expression of superior adaptation."[9]

The superiority theory of laughter is an attempt to explain that dimension of humor where people laugh at the misfortune of others and mock behavior that is reckoned to be inappropriate. This involves a wide range of types of humor extending from very gentle and friendly forms of jesting, wisecracks, and witticisms through to more combative forms of satire, sarcasm, and mockery as well as aggressive humor that offends and excludes. This form of humor can enhance relationships by demonstrating a commitment to friendship that is not fractured by pointing out people's inevitable frailties and inadequacies and, at the more intense level, it can reveal and challenge injustices and inappropriate behaviors. In some contexts a cartoon with an easily identifiable public figure who responds to the question "Do you know the Golden Rule?" with "Oh, yes, whoever has the gold makes the rules," might be mildly amusing while in a different political context it might well be considered politically subversive and dangerous. The prophets of ancient Israel used mockery to discredit opponents of God (1 Kgs 18:25–7) and God is described as laughing at those who oppose him (Ps 2:2–5). Thus some forms of this humor can be viewed positively, as having moral character despite the aggression involved. It can, of course, also be morally damaging when it is used as a way of hurting or excluding certain people and it can, at times, be ambiguous and perceived differently by those who hear it.

---

5. Hegel, *Philosophy of Fine Art*, 302.
6. Hazlitt, *Lectures on English Comic Writers*, Lecture 1.
7. Bain, *The Emotions and the Will*, 153.
8. Bergson, "Laughter," 149.
9. Ludovici, *The Secret of Laughter*, 74.

ing laughter "an expression of self-satisfied shrewdness";[5] the Englishman William Hazlitt (1788–1830) asserting that "we laugh at absurdity . . . at deformity . . . at mischief . . . at what we do not believe . . . to show our satisfaction with ourselves, or our contempt for those about us, or to conceal our envy or our ignorance";[6] the Scot Alexander Bain (1818–1903) arguing that laughter was occasioned in "everything where a man can achieve a stroke of superiority, in surpassing or discomfiting a rival";[7] and the Frenchman Henri Bergson (1859–1941), noting that "it is the trifling faults of our fellow-men that make us laugh."[8] In more recent times this view has adapted to evolutionary theory with Anthony M. Ludovici arguing that "all laughter is the expression of superior adaptation."[9]

The superiority theory of laughter is an attempt to explain that dimension of humor where people laugh at the misfortune of others and mock behavior that is reckoned to be inappropriate. This involves a wide range of types of humor extending from very gentle and friendly forms of jesting, wisecracks, and witticisms through to more combative forms of satire, sarcasm, and mockery as well as aggressive humor that offends and excludes. This form of humor can enhance relationships by demonstrating a commitment to friendship that is not fractured by pointing out people's inevitable frailties and inadequacies and, at the more intense level, it can reveal and challenge injustices and inappropriate behaviors. In some contexts a cartoon with an easily identifiable public figure who responds to the question "Do you know the Golden Rule?" with "Oh, yes, whoever has the gold makes the rules," might be mildly amusing while in a different political context it might well be considered politically subversive and dangerous. The prophets of ancient Israel used mockery to discredit opponents of God (1 Kgs 18:25–7) and God is described as laughing at those who oppose him (Ps 2:2–5). Thus some forms of this humor can be viewed positively, as having moral character despite the aggression involved. It can, of course, also be morally damaging when it is used as a way of hurting or excluding certain people and it can, at times, be ambiguous and perceived differently by those who hear it.

---

5. Hegel, *Philosophy of Fine Art*, 302.
6. Hazlitt, *Lectures on English Comic Writers*, Lecture 1.
7. Bain, *The Emotions and the Will*, 153.
8. Bergson, "Laughter," 149.
9. Ludovici, *The Secret of Laughter*, 74.

tion reveals that they are actually more foolish, not so able, or are lesser in some way. This is the foundation of what has generally become known as the superiority theory of laughter, although Plato's various comments do not really constitute a complete theory. This view of laughter as involving comparative superiority-inferiority sees laughter primarily as ridicule and has an aggressive edge to it, as well as an element of ethical judgment because the one who laughs has, or at least believes that he or she has, the moral high ground. Other forms of laughter exist in Plato's thought but they are not so important in defining the essence of laughter, because they are more the result of emotions which override rationality and self-control, which have high value for Plato.

In general terms Aristotle followed the same line, believing that laughter was based on feelings of superiority concerning that which was considered ugly, deformed, mistaken, or below average. But in contrast to Plato he was prepared to see a more positive dimension to other forms of laughter, which he saw as useful for relaxation and refreshment. He noted the comedic value of the unexpected and hinted at the role of incongruity in humor. There was, he felt, an appropriate level of laughter that fell between the extremes of humorlessness and buffoonery.[3] He remained reserved about the morality of humorists like satirists and writers of comedy, who he considered to be evil people.

These observations about laughter originating in a sense of superiority benefited from being a part of what became the philosophical foundation of Western thought and they were largely taken as given, even though they had to wait until the time of Thomas Hobbes (1588–1679) for them to be put into a theoretical framework. In his essay "Human Nature," Hobbes gave a psychological account of the person and their passions in which he defended the view that laughter is based on a comparative judgement of our own superiority: "I may therefore conclude that the passion of laughter is nothing else but a sudden glory arising from sudden conception of some eminency in ourselves, by comparison with the infirmities of others, all with our own formerly."[4] Hobbes also accepted that there were other aspects of laughter but they were secondary, he insisted that in laughter one *really* is dealing with jealousy, self-interest, and ridicule at the weakness of others. This continued the influence of the superiority theory among European philosophers with the German Georg W. F. Hegel (1770–1831) call-

---

3. Aristotle, *Nichomachean Ethics*, IV.4.
4. Hobbes, "Human Nature," 46.

This theory does explain certain forms of humor but it is far from adequate as an overall theory because not only does it not explain many other different forms of humor (such as absurdist or self-deprecating humor and many forms of wit), but it does not always even accurately explain the relationship between superiority and laughter. That is, feelings of superiority do not always lead to laughter, as when a person's awareness of their financial superiority over another leads to compassion rather than amusement, and not all aggressive or challenging humor comes about from a sense of superiority; it may be the result of frustration or annoyance. Francis Hutcheson (1694–1746) wrote *Reflections upon Laughter,* which was an early critique of Hobbes theory that sought to break the long-established identification of humor with a sense of superiority, an identification that had actually constrained more creative thinking about the essence of humor. Superiority theory is essentially an anti-social view of laughter and it is inevitable that laughter will ultimately be viewed with deep suspicion to the detriment of those very positive aspects of humor that are relegated to, at best, secondary status. Unfortunately, the long dominance of the superiority theory meant that the church inherited these more negative views of humor along with many other values of the ancient world. As the literary critic Ernst Robert Curtius (whose pioneering study on "European literature and the Latin Middle Ages" [1948] contains a short chapter on "The Church and Laughter") noted, "The ideal values of antiquity were taken over by early Christian monasticism."[10] Superiority theory militated strongly against any positive assessment of humor and especially of laughter as an element of divine joy.

Relief theory

At his father's funeral the bereaved son tells a funny story about his recently deceased father and everyone relaxes a little. After a tornado some home owners express their humor and resilience when they put up a sign saying, "House for sale: half off." In the operating room the medical team deal with its nerves with dark humor. People often joke to cover their nerves while waiting for the results of an exam or a job interview. These are all examples of the relief theory, which sees humor as a form of emotional or nervous relief that reduces stress or lightens the mood of an otherwise difficult situation. The laughter might be either the release of pre-existing nervous

10. Kuschel, *Laughter*, 470.

energy or emotional feeling, or it might be a feeling deliberately brought about by a comedian discussing a sensitive topic, creating a certain tension and then relieving it through laughter. Relief theory deals with humor that can emerge in situations dealing with very mild social niceties and in seriously solemn, sad, or potentially explosive situations. When compared with superiority theory it is soon clear that relief theory is much more focused on humor as an emotion and thus on the physiological and psychological dimensions of the laughter that is produced by this inner release. It is a theory that has thus developed in more modern times, compared with the more classic superiority theory, as there has been an ever-increasing focus on the inner life of the individual self.

Physiological interest in the origin and nature of humor, extending the much earlier work of Galen, was developed by Lauren Joubert's *Treatise on Laughter* (1579) and then Descartes' *The Passions of the Soul* (1649), both examining the movements of muscles, the role of the diaphragm, the flow of blood, and the explosive movement of air from the lungs. Although they included some material relating to what we refer to here as relief and incongruity theories they still also emphasized the classic superiority theory. Anthony Ashley Cooper's essay *The Freedom of Wit and Humour* (1711) also connected physiology with aspects of relief theory (as well as superiority theory). As was typical for his day he understood nerves to be tiny tubes carrying fluids (or "spirits") that caused the muscles to move through pressure. Shaftesbury argued that when some action or movement or desire was constrained by some other person or external force the fluids/spirits could relieve the pressure by laughing. This general way of thinking about feeling "pressure" and gaining "relief" or venting through laughter has remained long after the physiological understanding has changed. The notion that laughter is a venting of pressure in the nervous system was subsequently developed by Herbert Spencer and then by Sigmund Freud.

In his *On the Physiology of Laughter* (1860), Herbert Spencer developed the notion of laughter as the muscular release of nervous energy that occurs when feelings build up in us but then are seen to be wrong or inappropriate. He saw the important role of incongruity in humor but felt that it was not, alone, a sufficient explanation as not all incongruities are seen as funny. Laughter only follows if there is an incongruity that shifts the emotions to a lower state of arousal, producing an excess of nervous energy that is then discharged in laughter.[11] Freud wrote about humor in his

---

11. Billig, *Laughing and Ridicule*, 88–91.

Jokes and Their Relation to the Unconscious (1905) and an essay "Humor" (1928). He followed Spencer with his own version of relief theory, in which he classified humor according to the kind of relief that it produced—nervous, mental, or emotional. In each case a certain form of mental energy is summoned up for a psychological purpose that is then is not required and so the superfluous energy is used in laughter. Joking, according to Freud, is where one explores those hostile or sexual feelings that, because of social constraints, usually be repressed. The *nervous energy* that would otherwise have been expended in repressing those feelings is now expressed in laughter. Because violence and sex are the two main sources of repressed nervous energy many jokes are about sex and violence. With the comic one is dealing with some situation that apparently requires *mental energy* to solve it, but then something unexpected happens and a solution is not required, the superfluous mental energy is now expressed in laughter. Humor involves a situation that appears to require an emotional commitment, such as sympathy or fear, for someone, which, in the end is not required and the *emotional energy* saved becomes humor.

In developing his psychodynamic approach to psychology, Freud wrote books on both dreams and jokes, but while the former was very influential the latter was not followed nearly so much, to the detriment of the study of humor. Jon Roeckelein notes that of 136 introductory psychology textbooks produced between 1885 and 1996 only three made any reference to humor or laughter at all and Mahadev Apte notes that most anthropology textbooks do not list humor as a significant part of cultural systems.[12] In more recent decades, however, there has been a renewal of interest. This has not led to a revision of the fundamental theories, but there has been work done on integrating them and work has been progressing on expanding the understanding of humor in many specific and previously unresearched areas. Cognitive neuroscience is being used to provide insights into the way that humor functions neurologically; evolutionary theorists have sought to explain humor and laughter in terms of its survival benefit; there has been work on the physiology of humor and its role in pain tolerance and physical health and well-being; there has been extensive psychological research on humor in human development, therapy, counseling, education, leadership, work, personality types, and many other areas, and there has been research into laughter and humor correlates in animals.

---

12. Roeckelein, *The Psychology of Humor*, 3; Apte, *Humor and Laughter*, 22.

Incongruity theory

The dominant theory of humor today is incongruity theory, which believes that humor lies in the observation of something that is incongruous or, taking a broad view of its meaning, unexpected, ambiguous, logically impossible, irrelevant, or inappropriate. Those who hold to it usually understand it to be not merely one, but to be *the* basic form of all humor. It is mentioned in Aristotle's observations but was not a full-blown theory in earlier times. The theory first really developed in the late eighteenth and early nineteenth centuries. According to Morreall the first to use the term "incongruous" to analyze humor was by James Beattie,[13] and the theory was soon developed in various ways by Immanuel Kant, Arthur Schopenhauer, Søren Kierkegaard, and William Hazlitt. It subsequently became, in its various forms, the dominant theory.

The central and potentially most problematic aspect of incongruity theory, however, is that incongruity *by itself* does not explain why things are funny. Some things that are incongruous almost inevitably produce laughter, but some things that are incongruous are definitely not funny, like a car designed for safe and comfortable travel lying crashed in a ditch with injured passengers. Other things, such as some works of art that distort reality in unexpected ways, are incongruous and interesting without being humorous. Clearly, there is something else involved in the perception of incongruity that has to be defined. The problem of not being precise about this is seen, for example, in Schopenhauer, who, in theory, saw humor as subjective and depending on a particular mood, while actually stressing the apparently obvious effect of just suddenly observing an incongruity. Consequently, his theory remains incomplete and some of his singularly un-funny examples demonstrate this. A drawing of a line running at a tangent next to a circle is, by itself according to Schopenhauer, humorous because at their closest point the lines are theoretically parallel, but they *look* as though they are at an angle. If this kind of visual joke was actually extended to be something more like one of M. C. Escher's optical illusions it might be funny, but Schopenhauer's version is unconvincing and in this and a number of other examples he demonstrates, inadvertently, the importance of the subjective element. In another example of humor he recounts the words on a gravestone erected by a poor black family that compared their tragically deceased child to a broken lily. An epigraph

---

13. Morreall, *Philosophy of Humor and Laughter*, 74.

comparing a poor, black, deceased child to a white lily is, to Schopenhauer, not only incongruous but also obviously silly and humorous. Schopenhauer is trying but, as Terry Eagleton observes, he "is a thinker so unremittingly gloomy that his work, quite unintentionally, represents one of the great comic masterpieces of Western thought."[14]

William Hazlitt discussed the fact that there are various responses to incongruity, including fear and sadness as well as laughter, and argued that the difference between them lay in *whether they were serious or trifling matters*: "We weep at what thwarts or exceeds our desires in serious matters: we laugh at what only disappoints our expectations in trifles."[15] This distinction contains an element of truth but is not sufficient. Sometimes this distinction applies but it is not always so. Some trifling incongruities are *not* funny and at times humor *is* found in the most and desperate serious circumstances. Søren Kierkegaard argued that the difference between a tragic and a comic view of incongruity (or, as he referred to it, of "contradiction") lay in whether there was a sense of hope in the assessment of the situation.[16] Hope is the ability to perceive a way through the situation and a comic approach to a difficult and serious situation can often be more creative, imaginative, insightful, and ultimately wiser than despair. To be able to laugh, or even offer a wry smile, in a difficult situation is an expression of faith and hope that all will, eventually, be well. For Kierkegaard the connection of hope with the comic means that of the three forms or philosophies of life that he examines—the aesthetic, the ethical, and the religious—the religious is intrinsically more comical. Consequently, the humorous is necessarily present throughout Christian faith. Hope means that the person has a fuller, more complete assessment of the incongruous situation, they are able to even laugh at themselves or at others for their foolishness, vanity, ignorance, weakness, or whatever frailty is demonstrated, rather than simply falling into despair. Laughter is a recognition of the true nature of the self, humanity, and the world.

---

14. See Schopenhauer, *The World as Will and Idea*, and Eagleton, *The Meaning of Life*, 82.

15. Morreall, *Philosophy of Humor and Laughter*, 65.

16. Kierkegaard, *Concluding Unscientific Postscript*, 459–68.

Play theory

Yet, seen from a theological point of view, there is even more to laughter than this. While it is, on the one hand, a recognition of the nature of the world and humanity, it is also a dynamic and joyful recognition of the almost incomprehensible nature of God and of the work of salvation. When one considers the world in the light of God one is faced with the greatest incongruity and the most profound contradiction. One who, through this, comes to a new understanding of God may be filled with a profound sense of awe and apprehension, but they may also, perhaps even more appropriately, be filled with praise and adoration, joy and laughter. And while the one who develops a new and deeper appreciation of what God has done in salvation to transform all the incongruities and contradictions of the world may well fall on their face in fear and trepidation when they consider their own sinful state, they may also, and perhaps even more appropriately, explode with laughter at the defeat of all forms of sin and evil and the eradication of all pain and suffering. Awe and apprehension, belief and baptism, confession and commitment, devotion and discipleship are all appropriate expressions of human response to the revelation of God's nature and work, but beyond all these there is laughter as an expression of joy, with the belly-laugh as the highest form of relationship with God. Indeed, it has been said that "Laughter is the closest thing to the grace of God."

This quotation, that laughter is the closest thing to the grace of God, is frequently attributed to the theologian Karl Barth both by scholars and popular writers. However, despite its wide currency and its obvious appeal it seems that Barth may not actually have said it. The popularity of the quotation seems to derive from its appearance in the *Harper Book of Quotations*[17] but that book does not provide a reference to any specific source in Barth and a search of the *Digital Karl Barth Library*[18] did not turn up the comment in anything Barth wrote. It seems possible to me that it is attributed to Barth in much the same way that Albert Einstein is used as an authoritative source for many apocryphal quotations, including, "The problem with quotes on the internet is that you can't always be certain of their accuracy." This, however, does not mean that Barth was uninterested in humor or that the oft-quoted passage does not represent something in his thought. The translator and interpreter of Barth, T. F. Torrance, was

---

17. Fitzhenry, ed., *The Harper Book of Quotations*.
18. *Digital Karl Barth Library*, https://dkbl.alexanderstreet.com/2018.

prepared to say that "Barth's humour played a fundamentally critical role in his thinking."[19] Barth was well known as a humorist in life and Heinrich Vogel wrote an extended piece on "The Laughing Barth."[20] In particular, humor influenced the manner in which Barth viewed the role of the theologian. He saw laughter as a recognition of human frailty and it meant that Barth was able to laugh at himself—he was always ready to see his own inadequacies and, as Torrance said, "he would never let himself become a prisoner to his own formulations."[21] It also meant that he was also able to rigorously critique, and laugh at, the ideas of others while appreciating their persons and their integrity. Barth notes that God laughs scornfully at those who oppose God's plans and encourages the faithful to do the same, especially when theologians suggest that "God is dead." The devil, he suggests, can only be dealt with with horror, contempt, resistance, and humor. Barth also endorses positive, joyful laughter and sees it as a mark of human uniqueness. Somewhat jocularly he distinguishes human life from that of animals by noting that only people laugh and smoke! People, he argues, should laugh and have their amusements and recreational activities but, as a Reformed scholar, he also wryly notes that John Calvin, the father of Reformed theology, had such an absolute devotion to the cause that he had no real amusements, little aesthetic sensibility, hardly ever took a holiday, and one has to search his works with a magnifying glass to find any evidence that he could laugh. An influence, he notes, that extends down to modern Reformed Protestantism.

At a deeper theological level a sense of humor is, for Barth, one aspect of the true humanity of Christ. Even though Scripture does not specifically describe Christ as laughing it is foolish to assume that he did not. At this point Barth comes to the heart of the matter when he observes that it is precisely the triune life of God that leads to divine laughter. It is nothing less than "this triune being and life," that is Godself, that is ultimately revealed as enlightening, persuasive, convincing, radiant, joyful, attractive, and beautiful. "The triunity of God is the secret of His beauty. If we deny this, we at once have a God without radiance and without joy (and without humour!)"[22] God is joyful and there is an appropriate human laughter that comes in response to the divine life and work. There is the laughter of

19. Torrance, *Karl Barth*, 12. Also see Ramm, "The Laughing Barth," 193–97.
20. Vogel, *Der lachende Barth*, 64–71.
21. Torrance, *Karl Barth*, 13.
22. Barth, *Church Dogmatics* IV, Part 3.1; 661.

genuine faith and also a very appropriate "Easter laugh." Barth perhaps comes closest to the quotation attributed to him, "Laughter is the closest thing to the grace of God," in a discussion of the nature of faith which he describes laughter as "human gratitude for the grace shown by God." Such faith, he says, is comparable to the natural development of a bud into a flower, the natural inclination of this flower toward the sun, and to "the natural laughter of a child."[23] Faith is thus likened to laughter, a joyful response to God's grace. In the end, although Barth may have preferred to have slightly rephrased the quotation that is widely attributed to him, he would have appreciated its basic intent to connect laughter with the character of the triune God.

That which theologians speak of as "the triune life of God" is an expression of the biblical testimony to God who is Father, Son, and Spirit, God whose inner life is expressed most completely in John's declaration that "God is love" (1 John 4:8). This inner life of love overflows in love for the world and the people that God has created and thus the truest form of relationship between God and humanity is not characterized by obedience or service so much as by love. God does not want servants who obey so much as friends who share, enjoy, appreciate, and laugh together. This is described further in *God is Friendship: a Theology of Spirituality, Community and Society,* where I develop a theology of friendship based on John 15:10–5 and especially the words "I no longer call you servants . . . but I have called you my friends." This theology of friendship and, subsequently, play and laughter, emerged unexpectedly as a result of considering the role of servanthood in the life of the Christian disciple. Servanthood has, in recent times, become a dominant model for the follower of Christ. It is taught, sung about, and widely accepted as the central image for believers to copy. But the situation in John 15 is that of Jesus speaking to his followers after they have shared their lives with him for several years and had learned much about his way of life. As Jesus said, "I have made known to you everything that I have heard from my father." Now it was time to make clear the kind of relationship that the mature disciple was to have with Christ. To those who "abide in his love" and "obey his commends," Jesus says, "I do not call you servants any longer . . . but I have called you my friends." Unfortunately much Christian teaching reverses the impact of this statement and assumes that while "friendship with Jesus" describes a good and loving relationship—an image especially suitable for children—that

---

23. Barth, *Evangelical Theology,* 103.

those who want to be serious about their faith, and those who are mature will focus upon the more difficult, demanding, and sacrificial idea of being a true servant or slave of Christ Jesus. Yet the words of Jesus are the reverse of this. Servanthood is what is expected of those who initially come to follow Jesus; friendship better expresses the warmth, the intimacy, the closeness and particularly of the grace involved in the relationship. God does not merely want servants but wants friends. God wants to enjoy the relationship that involves joy, playfulness, and laughter. Therefore, from a theological point of view laughter is part of the expression of the playfulness that is inherent in friendship with God.

This is a development of the incongruity theory of laughter. Humor certainly involves incongruity, but as has been noted, incongruity alone is not a sufficient explanation. This theological interpretation of laughter therefore is consistent with, but also a development of incongruity theory and better described as *a play theory of laughter*. The believer laughs as an expression of (a) their faith, which means having an awareness of the grace of God who wants to be their friend—something totally incongruous and unexpected, and (b) their hope, their certain conviction, that God is redeeming and resolving all of the incongruities and aberrations of the world.

The use of the concepts of friendship, play, and laughter as expressions of the most intimate and important forms of relationship with God is not completely unknown in Christian tradition, but it is extremely rare. Fortunately, these concepts do have their champions. In *Spiritual Friendship*, for example, Aelred of Rievaulx (1110–1167) produced one of the great works of medieval spirituality, though it was not nearly as influential as it should have been. Thomas Aquinas (1225–1274) was apparently unaware of Aelred's work when he produced a theology with God as Chief Friend[24] and he also used Aristotle's concept of *eutrapelia* ("playfulness") in order to develop his thoughts on the theological importance of playing with God.[25] But neither friendship nor play have been consistently been given the place, the theological and spiritual role, that they deserve. Nor, especially, has laughter. In the twentieth century, however, non-theological assessments of laughter have progressively attributed more and more positive outcomes to laughter.

In recent times laughter has overcome many of the philosophical reservations about its allegedly aggressive, irrational, and emotional nature that are found in superiority and relief theories and has largely gained

---

24. See Edgar, *God is Friendship*, 127.
25. See Edgar, *The God Who Plays*, 10–13, 60–61.

theoretical respectability as a result of being seen as having numerous physical, psychological, social, and creative benefits. Some of these utilitarian benefits may prove to be less significant than has been thought, but from a theological point of view that is largely irrelevant because the real purpose of humor is not to be found in these things. Theologically and spiritually laughter is simply a good in itself. It certainly is connected with, and comes about as the result of, the way that humor enables us to see ourselves and the world as it really is and it therefore is part of the process of lessening our own desire to control life. It teaches us to not take ourselves too seriously and it frees us from vanity. At the same time it gives us an accurate view of a flawed, inconsistent, often ambiguous and sinful world. All of this is extremely valuable and yet, even more significantly, laughter is an appropriate response to an ever deepening awareness of the nature and the work of God. God in Christ is the genuinely unexpected, the completely surprising, the totally incongruous one who is both transcendent and immanent, God and man, crucified and crowned, savior and sacrifice. This deserves great laughter that goes beyond all other hilarity and merriment. It is an act of joy that expresses one's faith, hope, and love. Indeed, as it has been said, "laughter is the closest thing to the grace of God."

9

Laughter at the Cross

Blessed are you who weep now,
for you will laugh

—Jesus Of Nazareth (Luke 6:21)

A theology which aims to locate laughter at the heart of the human relationship with God is obliged to explain the two most difficult dimensions of humor: its use in cruel mockery and the possibility of laughter in the midst of pain, evil, and suffering. With regard to mockery there is no doubt that laughter can involve a powerful and emotional critique of a person or group. It can be so cruel that some do not see it as humor at all, nonetheless it can be a just and appropriate response, one that points to the seriousness of some unjust and cruel actions—just as God mocks the unrighteous and those who deliberately ignore his commands (Prov 1:26 and 3:34; Jer 10:15). But those who engage in mockery must themselves be very careful as mockery can be the result of self-righteousness. There are a number of biblical warnings, especially in Proverbs, about those who have become mockers, who are identified with the proud, the arrogant, and the foolish (Prov 13:1; 15:12; 19:29; 21:24).

Laughter and the cross

Mockery was a prominent part of the abuse that culminated in the crucifixion of Christ. It seemed to a number of people that certain claims concerning Christ were false and deserving of mockery. Casual passersby mocked Christ by observing that if he could be said to have saved Lazarus and others from death that he ought to be able to save himself by coming down from the cross. The soldiers scoffed at the claims that he was a prophet by saying that he therefore ought to be able to know who it was that was striking him. Pilate and the soldiers mocked the claim that he was a king by dressing him in royal robes and a crown of thorns, saluting him and kneeling before him, and they placed a sign over his head saying, "The king of the Jews" (Mark 15:16–25; Luke 22:63). The act of crucifixion itself was a cruel form of mockery reserved for those who behaved, according to Roman law, as though they had more rights and power than they actually did, generally non-citizens such as slaves and rebels and other enemies of the empire.

However, the warning found in the Wisdom literature that the mocker must be careful because they may end up being the one mocked comes to fruition when the mockers and scoffers of Christ find that the joke is really on them! There is mockery of the mockers because it turns out that the foolishness of the gospel—"Christ and him crucified"—is actually the power of God (1 Cor 2:1–4). His mocking "enthronement" is actually a demonstration of his genuine kingship. The one who appeared to be subject to death is resurrected and takes on immortality and death is "swallowed up in victory," so that Paul can rhetorically ask, "Where, O death, is your victory? Where, O death, is your sting?" (1 Cor 15:50–5). This produces great laughter and it should be noted that there are two parts to it.

Firstly, there is positive joy and laughter at the fact of the resurrection, the laughter of the redeemed who, as brothers and sisters of Christ, receive eternal life themselves. Secondly, there is mocking laughter at death, the evil one, and everything that sought to make people subject to sin, slavery, and death. Jürgen Moltmann says this laughter displays human freedom from the rulers of this age; it is the "beginning of the rebellion of the liberated against the bonds of their slavery."[1] Gregory of Nyssa (c. 330–c. 396) made mocking laughter at the devil an important aspect of his theory of redemption, in which the divine nature of Christ was hidden under his human form that was a bait for the devil to seize. His divinity was the hook on which the devil was then caught as he gulped down the divinity of Christ, along with the bait of his human nature, so that the life and light of Christ were taken into the world of the evil one and they overcame both darkness and death.[2] This was an image of the atonement that was followed by others

---

1. Moltmann, *Theology and Joy*, 51.
2. Gregory of Nyssa, "Great Catechism," ch. 24.

such as Maximus the Confessor and it achieved a high level of popularity in the medieval church. The idea of laughing in mockery at the devil and laughing in joy at the resurrection was certainly a medieval practice, albeit sometimes abused and often controversial. The *risus paschalis*—the Easter laugh—became a part of the liturgy of the church.

One Catholic version of this tradition that originated in Bavaria in the fifteenth century involved the priests inserting funny stories into their sermons and scathing descriptions of the devil's vain attempts to keep the doors of hell locked against Christ who came to free the captives. In medieval France at Auxerre in the twelfth century, Easter worship involved a decorated church, the bishop dancing, and ball games for all. The dean would carry a ball in the procession into the sanctuary and on reaching the altar, would also dance. There is a ritual for vespers from Besancon dating from 1528 that includes dancing and the distribution of wine. This was held on or around New Year's Day. At around the same time in Vitre on the Feast of St. Stephen there was a custom of elevating a ball, which had been placed on the altar for that purpose, during the mass, between the elevation of the chalice and the host.[3]

In the opinion of some at least, it got a little out of hand as it led to some rather curious interpretations of Scripture and exaggerated behavior. Before becoming a noted Reformer, Oeclampadius (1482–1531), a priest in Basel, was very critical of the foolish and sometimes smutty humor that was then part of the Easter celebration. The jokes of other preachers "banish in every way the piety and gratitude towards God that we should increase."[4] The story of the resurrection could become a comedy play in which there is burlesque byplay involving the wife and the servant of a shopkeeper who sells Mary ointment while on her way to the tomb. It could turn the apostles' rush to the tomb into a comic race and have the risen Christ appearing as a gardener who suggests to Mary that she might be in the garden to meet her lover. Oeclampadius complained that it gets to the point where the preacher is like "a travelling comedian," which he felt was shameful and frivolous.[5] The practice was banned in the seventeenth century by Clement X and in the eighteenth by Maximilian III and the bishops of Bavaria.[6]

---

3. Rahner, *Man at Play*, 78–87.
4. Kuschel, *Laughter*, 84–85.
5. Ibid., 85.
6. Holweck, "Easter."

The general expectation of the era was that the religious life was based on asceticism, self-denial, and sacrifice, and it is perhaps only to be expected that this could produce some outbursts of humor that released the inevitable pressure of the usual community expectations. Karl-Josef Kuschel claims that "in the Middle Ages there was no theology of laughter, but there was a theology of tears."[7] This is an expression of the approach that was approved by John Chrysostom, who spoke of a theology of tears on the basis that Scripture does not speak of Christ, Paul, or the other apostles as laughing but as weeping. This present life, he argued, is not the theater for laughter.[8] Kuschel's claim is perhaps an overstatement, although representing the majority view of the religious who were committed to an ascetic theology that had no role for laughter in the spiritual life, over lay people and some religious, who found a real place for "the Easter laugh" and related humor in their devotion. There was at least popular, if not religious, support for the Christian carnival, which stressed the place of the material, the worldly, the sensual, and the physical, including laughter.

Laughter and the evil one

The carnivalistic laughter of the *risus paschalis* expressed both positive and negative dimensions of humor. That is, it expressed the joyful laughter of the cross and the resurrection as well as the mockery of death and all the powers that sought to oppress humanity. The first of these, joyful laughter, is easier to comprehend, coming, as it does, as a response to the news of the resurrection of Christ and the promise of the general resurrection. But there is also great joy and laughter in the cross itself, and not only in the resurrection that follows it. There is laughter in the midst of the pain of the cross because it was there that Christ gave himself for others and won salvation for the world. There is laughter because it is the concrete expression of joy. Laughter is not always evidence of joy (it can be more superficial than that) but the absence of laughter is a sign of the absence of joy. True joy inevitably produces laughter and the cross, as well as the resurrection, is the central cause of Christian joy.

The mocking laughter which is part of the *risus paschalis* also comes as a result of the death and resurrection of Christ and has its biblical foundation in Paul's mockery of death, "Where, O death, is your victory?

---

7 Kuschel, *Laughter*, 48

8. Chrysostom, "Homilies on Matthew," Homily VI.6.

Where, O death, is your sting?" (1 Cor 15:55) and it is an important recognition that death, sin, and evil are finished, at an end and that any pretense that they are still powerful is a joke. Because the power of sin and death has been broken, congregations, pastors, preachers, theologians, and all believers can be confident in their salvation and can laugh at everything and anything that appears to be a threat to it. It is possible to laugh at one's own foolishness and at those who suggest in any way that material or spiritual things have the power to take us away from God. It also legitimizes laughing at the alleged power of the evil one and any power or injustice that pretends to be able to overcome Christ. They should not be taken seriously but scorned and rejected because they are defeated. In this way laughter becomes an important part of the Christian approach to evil, which, as a result of the work of Christ, may now be treated as a kind of joke. This does not, in any way, detract from the seriousness of sin and evil; it is rather intended to point to its inherent absurdity, its futility and foolishness, and to its ultimate nature as an unreal entity that has not merely been overcome but that has been eliminated.

This mocking approach is the way of Elijah in regard to the prophets of Baal and of Isaiah in regard to those who worship idols. The prophets of Baal declared that Baal was a god with great power and so Elijah challenged not merely the prophets, but Baal, to a competition to see who could "answer by fire" and miraculously light a fire that would burn a sacrifice. The inability of Baal to respond to the desperate pleadings of the prophets of Baal led Elijah into great mockery of their god who, he suggested, must be too deep in thought, or traveling or sleeping or perhaps in the toilet. The point of this mockery is to demonstrate not merely that Baal has no power but that Baal does not exist (1 Kgs 18:16–39). The same point is made by Isaiah in regard to the one who worships manufactured idols. The carpenter, for example, divides a block of wood in two, and one part of it is used as fuel for the fire to warm himself and to cook his food, while with the other part he carefully carves an idol in human form that he then proceeds to worship. He warms himself with one part of the wood, and when in trouble bows down to the other part and asks it to save him. "A deluded heart misleads him: he cannot save himself, or say, 'Is not this thing in my hand a lie?'" (Isa 44:1–20). The idol is not merely weak but a delusion, a construct of the imagination and the person who believes otherwise is to be laughed at.

This view of the false gods as delusions is one part of a paradox concerning everything that stands in opposition to God. They are presented as both real and unreal, as genuine and as impossible. The evil one is a tempter, a threat and a power (Matt 5:37; 6:13; John 17:15; 2 Thess 3:3; 1 John 2:13–4) but, at the same time, is defeated, unreal, and powerless. Now that Christ has achieved his victory the presence of sin and evil in the world is an incongruity that is, as Karl Barth says, "an ontological impossibility" that nonetheless has a form of reality.[9] The philosophical dimensions of this, which are so well discussed by Augustine, Barth, and others, have their practical outworking in the way the believer actually deals with the presence of these putative powers and in that regard there is no better source than Paul's discussion of spiritual warfare in Ephesians 6. His instructions are to "be strong in the Lord and in his mighty power" and to put on "the full armor of God" in order to stand against "the rulers, the authorities, the powers of this dark world and against the spiritual forces of evil." This confrontational approach is often misunderstood because the weapons that he says are to be used mean that this is not a battle fought on the enemy's terms. Indeed, given the description of the battle ahead the methods to be employed are totally incongruous. It is true that the armor and weapons described are those of a soldier of the day (armor, belt, breastplate, helmet, and sword) but they are interpreted in very nonconfrontational and extremely non-militant terms. They represent truthfulness, righteousness, peace, faith, and the word of God. The point is that the ways of the powers are to be ignored. Believers are to focus on the way of Christ and if they are faithful and righteous and live according to the gospel of peace then evil has no power over them and can be ignored. Their alleged power is nonexistent and whatever has to be done to defeat them has been done in Christ. This is a reason for laughter, on the one hand as that most devastating critique of the weakness of an opponent, and on the other hand as an expression of great joy at what God has done. The lesson is not to attribute too much strength to the opposing powers.

Laughter and lament

One might well laugh in the face of the evil one, but what about in the face of other aspects of our distorted world, such as pain and suffering? Is laughter an appropriate, theological part of the human response to death

---

9. Barth, *Church Dogmatics*, IV, Part 3.1; 68.

and disaster? The appropriateness of the way that anyone responds to tragedy at any one moment is, of course, not to be judged by others. It is a very personal and variable matter and all manner of responses including sadness, grief, anger, and feelings of desolation may occur. But is it possible for there to be laughter as well as lament right in the midst of suffering? For the believer there is the conviction that the resurrection of Christ is simply the first fruits of a resurrection and transformation of all, as well as the promise that there will come a time when God will be with his people and "He will wipe every tear from their eyes. There will be no more death or mourning or crying or pain, for the old order of things has passed away" (Rev 21:3–4). There is thus a real basis for hope, but that is grounded in future events and the question of the possibility and appropriateness of laughter in present times of trouble remains problematic. It is obvious that at times, people do find relief and release in laughter in the midst of difficulty, at funerals, and in the midst of tragedy. Some, for example, advocate laughing at cancer as a way of relating to this aggressive form of illness. This is a fundamentally different way of approaching cancer compared with the now well established imagery of battling it. There would hardly be a report of death from cancer that did not refer to the person's passing after "their long/short battle with cancer," which assumes a certain attitude towards the way that life is lived with this disease. There need be no diminution of the desire to overcome the cancer even if a person and perhaps a family determine to laugh through it. Humor is one way that many have coped with trauma and there have been, for example, significant studies on the importance of humor for those suffering the effects of the holocaust.[10] Not that there is any expectation that anyone ought to respond in a particular way—that is up to the individual, and, as Ecclesiastes reminds us there is a time for everything, including "a time to weep and a time to laugh."

- But when humor *is* found in tragedy is it merely *a diversion* from the problem, an opportunity to actually avoid the trauma for a few moments? Or is it actually a way of *relating to* it, an approach that has a more intrinsic connection with the pain itself?
- One might also contrast seeing humor as *a therapy which counters* the negative effects of suffering, with an approach which sees humor as a *theological validation* of one's fundamental attitude to all the effects of evil.

10. Ostrower, "Humor as Defense Mechanism."

The latter approach in each case suggests a more intimate connection between laughter and lament, something that might well be demonstrated, although perhaps not fully explained, through an examination of one of the books of the bible most commonly associated with lament about life's tragedies—the book of Job.

Laughter and Job

I felt somewhat guilty when I read that most excellent theorist of humor, John Morreall, saying that "it is difficult to imagine the reader who would react to the story of Job with laughter"[11] because that is exactly what I had been doing for quite some time. But if Morreall saw no humor there then perhaps *my* sense of humor was out of place! The story of Job, after all, is widely considered to be a tragedy, an exposition on the nature of human suffering with Job as a case study. And a profoundly tragic one at that, involving a most horrific sequence of events with, first of all, Job's oxen and donkeys taken by the Sabateans and the servants killed, then fire falling from heaven that kills his sheep and the servants, and then the Chaldeans steal his camels and kill more servants. This is then followed by news of the death of his sons and daughters in the collapse of their house and, finally, Job is covered with painful sores. I understand that practically everyone sees this solely as tragedy and so I was somewhat relieved to find that William Whedbee had previously argued that there *was* indeed humor in Job. His was very much a minority opinion but I agreed with him as I had always thought that at least the first couple of chapters of Job were hilariously funny and I regularly sought to persuade students that seeing the humor was important if one wished to understand the true nature of the relationship between God and satan that the book was putting forward. I had not, I concede, previously pursued the notion of comedy in the rest of Job, in the advice of his friends and the words of God, but now I think that failing to do so creates a certain inconsistency in the message of the book. Humor is actually important throughout. Not only does a comedic form not rule out there being a serious message, the comedy is actually to be seen as an important part of the message itself. The humor is more than a means of making the message more bearable. It is, more precisely, part of what the book of Job wants the reader to understand about tragedy.

11. Morreall, *Comedy, Tragedy, and Religion*, 99.

LAUGHTER AT THE CROSS

Humor in the dialog between God and satan

Those who begin their reflections on Job's sufferings at the point where disaster falls on him miss the significance of the first chapter involving the dialogue between God and satan that is "the set-up" for the whole book.

The story begins with basic detail about Job as a blameless and upright man who feared God and shunned evil. He had seven sons and three daughters and he continually made sacrifice for them, and he had many, many sheep, camels, oxen and donkeys, and numerous servants. He was "the greatest man among all the people of the East." With that situation established, the scene then abruptly shifts from Job to the angels with the statement that, "One day the angels came to present themselves before the Lord, and satan also came with them." This appears to be a picture of "the hosts of heaven" (1 Kgs 22:19) gathering before God. The heavenly host was comprised of nonhuman entities including messengers or angels, slaves, gods, or spirit and stars, as well as the assembly of the holy ones. God is, of course, the absolute Lord of this assembly, which even includes, under his authority and control, the somewhat puzzling satan whose apparent aim was to undermine those of God's people who behaved in an unrighteous way.

It may be that there is a sense in which satan is an interloper (in addition to the gathering of the angels it is noted that "satan also came with them," and there is the subsequent challenge, "Where have you come from?") and yet it must also be noted that satan's presence and participation is accepted. It is difficult not to attach to satan ideas of the devil that come from later literature and while a connection is not inappropriate the present account of the part satan plays in this drama must stand as it is. Satan here has an ambiguous role as part, albeit perhaps a questionable part, of the heavenly assembly of all spiritual, nonhuman beings that are subject to God. As such, satan is able to dialog with God and debate matters, even though satan's intent is perceived as unfriendly. Satan is not a personal name, it is better expressed as "the satan" or "the accuser" and his title points to his sole power, which is to accuse people of their unrighteousness. The satan is able to prosecute people but cannot determine their fate, which is God's prerogative. The first very important point to make here is to reiterate that fact that the satan has absolutely no power over any of God's people except the power to accuse them before God of the wrong that they have done. Satan has no power at all over those who are holy, obedient, and righteous. This reinforces the point made above concerning Paul's advice in Ephesians 6 about the weapons that will defeat the evil one. The second important point to derive from this story is that the satan acts only under the authority of God. Even the satan's limited power of accusation is only possible with the acquiescence of God who watches over his people. In like manner in Luke 22:31–4 the satan asks "to sift" Simon Peter and this request is, apparently, granted, although the Lord Jesus prays that he will be delivered through it. There is a sense in which, under the jurisdiction of God, the satan acts like a state prosecutor as the means to strain out impurities in the people of God.

Satan's role is paradoxical. The satan is both part of the assembly of heaven, a servant of God who is subject to divine control, and an accuser seeking out people's sins and apparently wanting to condemn them. A not unrelated issue concerning the ambiguous role of satan is found in a comparison of 2 Samuel 24:1 with 1 Chronicles 21:1, both of which describe the same situation—David's decision to conduct a census of Israel. While the writer of 2 Samuel says that it was "the anger of the Lord" that incited David to take this action, the writer of 1 Chronicles says that it is the case that "satan rose up and incited David." The problem is that precisely the same action is attributed to both God and to satan. If one leaves aside attempts to amend the text in order to harmonize the accounts (that have little support) one is left with a serious theological issue. Is God being confused with satan? Can they both be said to do the same thing? Or perhaps we are left with the same understanding of satan that Job presents (i.e., not some later understanding of satan as influenced by other literature and other theological content), whereby the satan can be seen as acting under the authority of God and being one of the means by which God achieves divine purposes. No doubt this will continue to raise other theological issues that lie beyond the scope of this book, but at this point we are only concerned with illuminating the identity and role of the entity referred to as satan in the book of Job. This satan does not have independent authority. In the end, however hard it is to understand given what happens to Job, God is in control.

With this understanding of the satan in mind it is now possible to ask about the way in which this short dramatic scene is presented. The angels come before God and the satan comes with them. The question "Where have you come from?" which, as noted above, could indicate that the satan is an interloper, is rather curious and the reader, or listener, is entitled to question the nature of the question. It is not exactly, "Why are *you* here?" (as though it was simply a challenge to satan's right to be present) and one may wonder whether God actually needed to be told where the satan had been just before arriving in the assembly. The question can, in fact, be read as a deliberate provocation of the satan and a challenge to the potency of his one and only power of accusation, because God knows *exactly* what satan has been doing and is actually setting things up to have some fun at the satan's expense. "So, satan, tell us where you have been . . ." But the satan is not very forthcoming about his recent activities because, as will soon become apparent, they have been embarrassing failures, and so he prevaricates with an obviously vague and inadequate response: "From roaming throughout the earth, going back and forth on it." One might imagine the satan shuffling his feet, looking down and around—anywhere but at God—and declaring, "Oh, I've just been hanging around, here and there. You know how it is." The satan's problem is that he, the accuser, is acutely embarrassed that he has no one to accuse! That is his role, and he has failed in it. Perhaps the assembly was smiling at this point; in any event, the understanding reader is certainly grinning at satan's discomfort. But God is not going to let the satan off the hook and get away with such dissembling and so he presses the point by asking, "Have you considered my servant Job?" And God knows full well that the satan will be further unsettled by this because Job is irreproachable. At this point the satan realizes that he is on a losing streak and decides to switch to attack and so he declares how unfair God is being (does anyone pity the satan in this?) because God is so good and kind to Job! (a point which hardly encourages sympathy for the satan). God has blessed Job, who now has flocks and herds and servants and a happy family. But if God were to really strike at Job and take all that away then surely Job would curse God and give the satan something to accuse him of! Satan is not coming across as an attractive character. But, as in any good drama, even one as short as this, the humor that the audience would have felt at the satan's discomfort is now suddenly challenged. The laughing mockery that was expressed at his failure is now replaced by the shock that comes when God declares that in the light of the satan's challenge that "everything he has is in your power." With the only proviso being that "on the man himself do not lay a finger." And so Job falls into the power of satan. Heavens above, that was not expected! What will happen now?

Humor in the tragedy of Job's life

What follows is an account of disaster after disaster for Job and it seems cruel to ask whether there is any humor in it, and yet given the preceding comedic context, can the description of the messengers coming with news of disaster be taken completely seriously? A lot depends on one's perception of the overall genre of the book and the extent to which it is a piece of literature carefully constructed to make a point concerning the nature of suffering rather than to describe an actual, specific situation. Scholars, however, have considerable difficulty gaining consensus in allocating Job to a particular genre. There is, nonetheless, despite the recognition of the irony of the book and instances of lighthearted descriptive material, a reluctance to categorize it as comedy. It does, however, seem to have a comic set-up in the account of the satan. Is there more to suggest some humorous intent?

William Whedbee is the pioneer in the claim that Job is a comedy and although subsequently there has been some recognition of aspects of humor in Job few have followed him completely, partly because of the related difficulties involved in ascertaining the genre and in discerning humor in another culture, but mainly because of the apparent conflict that comedy has with the theme of the nature and cause of suffering.[12] However, it is by no means impossible for humor and tragedy to coincide. In the wider literary world the possibilities inherent in tragicomedy are well understood. For example, there may well be a place for some comedic elements to lighten a play that might otherwise have been an unmitigated and oppressive tragedy. Or a piece dealing with very serious matters may have comedic elements and, as comedies always have—a happy ending. Job has at least four of the elements of a comedy. It certainly has both *a comic set-up* in the dialog with the satan, and the normal *conclusion* of a comedy—a happy ending with the Lord restoring Job's fortunes (seven more sons and three more daughters, just as previously, twice as much wealth as before, and good health to enable him to live to be twice the usual three score and ten years). The story also has, as will be shown below, comic *characters* in the form of his wife and his counselors as well as specific comic *content* in the way various people speak and behave. There is irony, hyperbole, foolishness, caricature, and laughter. Thus in structure, character, and content the book of Job has elements of humor. The likelihood, however, of the reader discerning the humor and reading events and people in comic rather than solely serious forms will depend very significantly on whether the reader actually believes that humor is intended and whether there is an implicit permission in the book itself for the reader to understand a comment as humorous or a character as a fool or a situation as ironic.

12. Whedbee, *The Bible and the Comic Vision*, and also see Pelham, "Job as Comedy."

LAUGHTER AT THE CROSS

The account of Job's disasters in chapters 1 and 2 may be taken purely as tragic or perhaps as having a stylistic and slightly unreal quality about it. Not only in the use of symbolic numbers—seven sons and three daughters, 7,000 sheep, 3,000 camels—but also in the stylized structure of the two scenes and the four disasters. There is, for example, the precise repetition in chapter 2 of elements of chapter 1 including the way the angels and satan come before God, the dialog about where satan has come from and the question (again?) about whether the satan has considered Job. There is also the repetition in the description of the actual tragedies in chapter 1 where four messengers arrive one after the other describing the various disasters in exactly the same kind of way and all with the same conclusion, "And I am the only one who has escaped to tell you!" Without doubting for a moment that there are many people who have suffered extraordinary, repeated disasters, even worse than this, and accepting that the book of Job is dealing with extremely serious issues of suffering, this particular account could well be interpreted as being set up for literary and theological purposes. There is also the irony that is to become a major theme in the book concerning the cause of Job's misfortunes. It appears from the start that Job has suffered everything simply so that God can demonstrate to the satan the faithfulness of Job! It might well justify the Jewish joke about being the chosen people of God, "Please God, choose someone else!"

In all of this it is made explicitly clear that Job is faithful. And while it seems that he has a legitimate complaint to make against God it is specifically noted in the text that he does not do this. The reader is now in a privileged position, knowing both that Job is a man without sin, considered by God to be blameless, and that he does not impugn the character of God because of his suffering (1:1; 1:22; 2:3; 2:11). Job is thus a truly righteous man. At this point Job's wife makes her almost farcical contribution to the situation. She appears to believe that in the light of all the tragedies he is foolish for continuing to proclaim his innocence—he *must be* guilty—apparently indicating that she, like almost everyone else in the book, accepted the dominant Hebrew conviction that tragedy was produced by sin. Well, like everyone else she is going to be shown to be wrong in that. (Incidentally, this is a claim that avoids the logical corollary concerning her own innocence or guilt, as it was as much her children that died and she was now suffering the same poverty as Job, although without the skin disease; but she apparently saw no guilt in herself.)

Job's wife saw Job suffering because of sin, and saw no way out for him and so concludes that he might as well get it all over done with: "Curse God and die!" Her advice to the righteous Job is to give up all hope, to turn his back on his own integrity and upon God, to blaspheme and effectively commit suicide. Is this, as has sometimes been suggested, a sincere desire to see Job out of his misery? Or is it a misunderstanding of the character of both Job and God, and a foolish, hopeless attitude that stands in contrast with Job's resolute commitment to not impugn God? It may be that it is impossible to know with certainty from the small amount of text exactly what her presuppositions or her motives were, but there are a couple of other hints that this may be a form of farce. The first is that the fact that Job's other counselors are presented as somewhat foolish certainly makes the notion that his wife is one as well a definite possibility. The second is that a somewhat comedic reading of Job's wife would lead well into Job's response utilizing the common literary technique of catching the reader off his or her guard by suddenly turning away from comedy to make a serious point. Job's response contrasts with that of his wife as he calmly declares, "You are talking like a foolish woman. Shall we accept good from God, and not trouble?" (2:10). The sudden switch from foolery to calm rationality accentuates the point being made concerning that very human propensity to consider matters from just one point of view. But then it is on to more comedy as his "friends" bring him "comfort."

Humor in the dialog between Job and his counselors

The dialog between Job and his friends and other counselors is both long and complex in form and contains a number of important elements with the comic ones primarily relating to the speeches of Job's counselors. Job himself however does engage in what might be seen as parody. Psalm 8:4–6 asks, "What is mankind that you are mindful of them, human beings that you care for them? You have made them a little lower than the angels and crowned them with glory and honor. You made them rulers over the works of your hands; you put everything under their feet." Job 7:17–18, on the other hand, in frustration asks, "What is mankind that you make so much of them, that you give them so much attention, that you examine them every morning and test them every moment? Will you never look away from me, or let me alone even for an instant?" And in 12:13–25 there is a parody of the common refrain of the psalms concerning God's almighty power, although in this case divine power and wisdom leads God to create leaders and nations only in order to destroy them. "To God belong wisdom and power; counsel and understanding are his . . . What he tears down cannot be rebuilt; those he imprisons cannot be released. If he holds back the waters, there is drought; if he lets them loose, they devastate the land . . . He leads rulers away stripped and makes fools of judges. He makes nations great, and destroys them; he enlarges nations, and disperses them. He deprives the leaders of the earth of their reason; he makes them wander in a trackless waste. They grope in darkness with no light; he makes them stagger like drunkards." The psalms certainly declares that God will bring down those leaders and nations that oppose him, but in this version God seems to be doing that in a more general fashion.

Job's friends can and do, at times, behave as sensitive and helpful counselors (their initial patience and empathy is commendable, 2:11–3). Much of what they say represents traditional Hebrew theology (such as the fine description of God's salvation in 5:9–16), and they express convictions that turn out to be correct (the advice that all will be well in the end turns out to be right, 5:24–26; 8:6), but on the other hand as the dialogs progress they become foolish and bombastic. At the start Eliphaz's preamble may be seen as simple courtesy, but it is also a precursor of later circumlocutions that are more pompous than polite and they all certainly end up annoying Job intensely. They also exaggerate and caricature certain points of theology and, especially unfortunately, they misapply their theological convictions to Job's situation. The reader is intended to recognize, based on what is said about Job by the narrator, that the friends' advice about the chastening of the Lord of those who sin (4:8) simply does *not* apply to Job.

So the advice is less than helpful, it is perhaps foolish, but is it comic? It is perhaps easier to initially recognize comic intent in the case of Elihu, whose advice and manner appear to be presented in such a way as to confirm the growing conviction that these advisors are a bit of a joke. At the end of chapter 31 the three friends of Job described as being present at the start, Eliphaz the Temanite, Bildad the Shuhite, and Zophar the Naamathite (2:11) have all finished speaking, and it is also noted that "the words of Job are ended." Once they have all finished, who is left to speak but God? But no, wait a moment, here comes Elihu, who appears for the first time, an angry young man (32:5) who thinks he knows more than the three, older friends (32:6–9), and he spends a long time declaring that he has to speak without actually saying anything. This includes a not-so-eloquent reference to being so full of things to say that he is like a man just bursting to find relief by urinating (32:19-20). He may not have intended this analogy to be a commentary on the sweetness of what comes forth but no doubt some readers will make the connection for him. Elihu becomes increasingly ludicrous, misappropriating what others have said, exaggerating and caricaturing God. In some respects his theology does represent Hebrew theology of the day, including in regard to the relationship of sin and suffering, yet he misapplies it to Job of whom he wrongly asserts, "to his sin he adds rebellion," when Job is actually guilty of neither (34:37). It is not merely Job's questions but specifically Elihu's rant that finally leads to the Lord's intervention as God breaks into the middle of Elihu's speech with, "Who is this that obscures my plans with words without knowledge?" (38:1-2). Elihu will *not* do as God's representative. He has been considered a buffoon by many since the time of the early Fathers and his role as a comic character is not only found in what he says but in the way that he makes clear the comic intent of other aspects of the form, the structure, and the content of Job. He makes clear that this is a book about tragedy that has a comic approach to finding truth.

Humor in God's speeches

With the entry of God into the story the reader now expects a resolution of the issue that has been plaguing Job and his friends. Chapters 38 to 41 belong entirely to God but the irony is—and it is very ironic—that after all these long speeches by Job and his counselors that God now gives a speech that, in itself, does not resolve, or even address, the fundamental issue that they were debating! It is, initially at least, a massive non sequitur.

Job's view of himself, one confirmed by the narration, is that he is a blameless man, at least as far as he knows. He harbors no known sin and while accepting that sin is possible he wants God to explain to him what sin, if any, there is so that he can deal with it. He wants God to explain the sin that would justify the tragedy that he is suffering. Otherwise, how he can be blamed for what he cannot know or deal with? He has a fair point. What is implicit in this is the conviction that there is a connection, and that there *ought to be* a connection, between his suffering and having done something wrong. Job's counselors, along with much of the theology of the Hebrew Bible, share the conviction that there is a connection between his suffering and having done something wrong. The difference is that the counselors want Job to explain himself, to admit to his sin while Job wants God to explain himself and reveal any sin. But God does not resolve the issue. At least not directly.

Given the debate that has gone on, *what God does not say* in response to Job and his counselors, and the reason for (apparently at least) not addressing their concerns, has to be considered, as well as *what God actually does say*. In the first case God does *not* come forward with a list of Job's sins to justify the suffering that he has endured. Such a list would have satisfied them all and would, according to their theology, have explained everything. But it seems that such a list is irrelevant, although even that has to be assumed because even that is not said specifically. (Perhaps there *is*, after all, a hidden, mysterious connection between sin and suffering, but if there is, it is not one that God is going to make clear.)

The best that one can say is that God's answer indicates that in terms of what humanity needs to know there is absolutely no need to speculate on a connection between an individual's sin and their suffering. This, of course, is a radical departure from other well-known expressions of Hebrew Bible and theology, as well as that found in Luke's account of common assumptions concerning the cause of death of certain Galileans that Pilate had killed, and the eighteen people killed when the tower of Siloam accidentally fell down (Luke 13:1–4). Jesus rhetorically asked those who were discussing these events whether they thought that these people were killed by Pilate or the falling tower because they were worse sinners than other Galileans or other people in Jerusalem at the time. His own answer was "I tell you, no!" and in so doing he, like the book of Job, broke any theological connection between individual sin and suffering. That is, it is wrong to suggest that a person's suffering results from their personal sin. But Jesus then took a different, though not contradictory, step to the words of God in the book of Job. In the latter case, as we shall see, the focus falls on the state of the *natural* world, but Jesus spoke more about *moral* connections. Having severed the connection between an individual's sin and suffering he then returns to it by saying, "But unless you repent, you too will all perish." That is, there *is* a connection between sin and death, although not on the basis of an individual's sin bringing immediate suffering or death. Even though there is no simplistic one-to-one correlation between individual sin and personal suffering this does not rule out a broader and more corporate relationship. The point is that sin that is not dealt with has potentially significant eschatological consequences, rather than consequences that can be observed in the present age.

In the book of Job, however, God simply does not address the issue of the corporate connection of sin and present-day consequences, thereby suggesting that both Job and his counselors had got it wrong. What he *did* do was to put forward a barrage of questions about the origin of the universe, the nature of the world, the causes of various natural events, the laws by which things operate, and the behavior of many kinds of animals. These are questions that Job, of course, is completely unable to answer. Yet, perhaps surprisingly, Job declares himself satisfied and his issues are resolved. God spoke of the natural world that he created, sustains, and nurtures, the world that God cares for, interacts with, and in which God may be found. This is the world that appeared terrifying and threatening to Job and that produced pain and loss and suffering, but it is also the world that God controls and cares for. It may contain pain but fundamentally it is God's world and he loves it and preserves it. It is, in fact, as presented in God's words, an unthreatening world that echoes with laughter and play. Animals are frequently associated with laughter, such as the joyful but rather silly ostrich who, when she runs, is so fast that she "laughs at horse and rider" who simply cannot keep up. The leviathan rules the sea and there is an extended description of the ridiculousness of a man trying to catch such a massive creature with a small fishhook, the unlikeliness of it being worried by anyone, and the impossibility of having it as a pet. The wild donkeys roam freely and happily and laugh at the people and the commotion of the town. The strong, free, and happy horse laughs at fear while the behemoth plays in the hills, secure and happy.[13] In the presence of a joyful, laughter-filled world that God has created and controls Job's worries simply melt away.

The speeches of Job's counselors are definitely comic, and Job himself indulges in irony, so is God's speech comic in any way? The fact that it does not address the issues that have been debated so intently for so long is undoubtedly ironic. The reader is inevitably taken aback by the focus of the divine speeches compared with those of Job and his counselors. The surprise is accentuated by the way that the speeches are dragged out and are sometimes nothing other than long-winded, but if one persists one finally arrives at . . . somewhere other than one could ever have expected, with thirty-five chapters of debate completely ignored by God. The irony of the situation then gives way to a joyful, delightful presentation of the natural world with animals leaping and frolicking and laughing and playing. This is

---

13. Job 39:13–8; 41:1–11; 39:5–8; 39:22; 40:20.

certainly different to the intense moral debate of earlier chapters. Are God's speeches comic? In their own gentle way, absolutely.

Humor in the epilogue

A happy ending does not, of itself, make a narrative a comedy, but a comic narrative really needs a happy ending. In this case there is the restoration of Job's fortune, reunion with his family and friends, the birth of seven more sons and three more daughters and a life lived to 140. This confirms the comic dimension of the narrative and the theological conviction that all will be well in the end, that God's salvation is real and will ultimately bring joy and laughter to all.

Suffering, humor, and growth

To many people, including as noted earlier to humor theorist John Morreall, it is surprising, even scandalous, to associate humor with the apparently terrible suffering described in the book of Job. And generally in life pain and suffering are more closely associated with grief and lament than with jokes and laughter. That seems to be the natural order of things. But our examination of Job reveals a surprising amount of humor of various types. There is humor in the dialog between God and satan that brought about the suffering (virtually for the sake of a bet!) and there is humor in the way that the tragedy of Job's life is presented. There are many absurdities and exaggerations in the advice given to Job by his friends, irony in God's response which does not deal directly with the questions asked, and joy at the full restoration of all the good things of Job's life at the end. There is a comic dimension to Job such that one might well conclude that the book—especially the advice of Job's counselors—has been taken a good deal more earnestly than is warranted.

The connection between the comic and the tragic has been noted in many other places including, for example, studies of the holocaust and at other times of significant tragedy. Motivational speaker and stand-up comic Judy Carter was due to start a promotional tour for her recently published book *The Comedy Bible* in front of 200 people in a comedy club in New York on September 13, 2001.[14] That is, forty-eight hours after the

14. Carter, *The Comedy Bible*.

tragedy of 9/11. Would it be funny to tell jokes at that time in a city that was stunned and grieving? There is always a short gap of time between the punch line of a joke and the audience reaction, and this is usually fairly short, though it varies with the topic and the joke's complexity, but on that night the gap in the first jokes seemed very long, but the laughter came and grew and developed. It was as though it was a declaration that humor is not to be taken away by disaster, that life does not end with tragedy, but life is comic with laughter winning over grief. This is a statement of faith and confidence in life and humanity and for the Christian there is, in addition, the confidence in the work of God both in the cross itself and in all that lies on the other side of the cross. That is, there is laughter *beyond* the cross because of the resurrection of Christ but there is also laughter *in* the cross itself (or, as Michael Screech puts it, "there is laughter at the foot of the cross"). This laughter *in* the cross is not only the negative kind of the mockery of death found in the apostle Paul's scathing cry, "Where, O death, is your victory? Where, O death, is your sting?" (1 Cor 15:55) but also the more positive humor involved in rejoicing at the salvation that comes from the fact that it is precisely the death of Christ that redeems the world. It is this that means that suffering itself has a positive and good dimension to it. It is not merely the fact of enduring to the other side of suffering is good, but suffering itself can be transformed into that which is good. Suffering can be a means to encourage others (2 Cor 1:4, 6, 9) and to lead Christians to care for others (2 Cor. 11:28, 30). It can lead to repentance (2 Cor 7:8) and enable a witness to non-Christians (2 Cor 6:4). It helps in the spread of the gospel (Phil 1:12; 2 Tim 2:8–10; Acts 5:40; 8:3) and can be a discipline (Heb 12:2–6, 11). It can lead to maturity (Jas 1:3), be a blessing (Matt 5:10–2; 1 Pet 3:14, 17) and, most importantly, it is a way to be like Christ (Phil 3:10; Col 1:24–29). Laughter is part of one's relationship with God and humor is a means to gaining wisdom and being like Christ. The faithful hear and understand the words of the Lord Jesus, "Blessed are you who weep now, for you will laugh" (Luke 6:21).

10

The Comic Christian Life

Taking ourselves too seriously deals a lethal blow to holiness.
—Doris Donnelly[1]

The spiritual and theological importance of laughter does not lie in its utilitarian value as a relief-giving, social-bonding, health-producing, trauma-relieving, psychologically beneficial, injustice-exposing phenomenon. No, its importance to the Christian does not lie so much in the good that humor does, but more in what humor *is*—as an essential, central dimension of the believer's relationship with God. Laughter is not a mere addition, or a kind of optional, added bonus to an otherwise genuine and sincere relationship, but rather an intrinsic, spontaneous, and joyful revelation of the nature, the depth, and the ecstasy involved in communion with God. It is an act of praise and an expression of faith. It is the deepest relationship we have with God. Humor can thus be seen as an essential part of the way to salvation and the nature of that salvation is made clearer as one specifically observes the connection. Some traditions describe the Christian life in terms of the *ordo salutis*—the order of salvation—which outlines a logical, though not necessarily chronological, process of change, such as Calling, Repentance, Justification, Regeneration, Sanctification, and Perfection. I did consider suggesting that there ought to be a specific place where Laughter is included, emphasizing its role as an essential part of life with God. But I decided against that because laughter is not something to be found in one place alone (and, anyway, it would likely just lead to debate about whether laughter ought to come before or after sanctification, in the

---

1. Donnelly, "Divine Folly," 392.

same way that there are debates about whether regeneration comes before repentance or not!). The following material does, however, note the connection between laughter and ten of the principal elements of the gospel of salvation and this will serve as an appropriate conclusion to our study of the theological and spiritual role of laughter. Humor, it will be seen, is theoretically important in the assessment of rational and paradoxical claims about God and practically significant as an essential element of divine love. Humor is also closely connected with humility, holiness, and the creative human imagination. It is an important part of the growth of Christian community and, for individuals, significant in developing hope and overcoming melancholy, depression, despair, and anger. Humor influences the way ministry is performed and is a part of the process of developing spiritual maturity. Finally, it is an element of the Apostle Peter's declaration concerning humanity's "participation in the divine nature."

Love and laughter

The most fundamental connection lies in the relationship between laughter and *the love of God*. Laughter is at the heart of it because as Agnes Repplier says, "We cannot really love anybody with whom we never laugh."[2] One may have other forms of relationship without humor or laughter of any kind but it is hard to conceive of a relationship of love that is devoid of it. At a purely human level the ability to laugh is one of, if not the most, valued qualities in relationships with life partners. It is prominent in what people seek when looking for a partner, significant in determining relationship satisfaction during the relationship, and important in what they say when eulogizing partners after their death. A purely work-related business partnership or a political alliance may well exist without a shared sense of humor (though it might be enhanced by one), but a relationship involving any intimacy or emotional feeling necessarily involves some humor. And this humor and laughter is not to be seen as additional to, or a consequence of, the relationship, it is, in a very real sense, a part of the relationship itself. Similarly, a shared sense of humor with God is a part of one's relationship with God. Laughing together is as important for this relationship as it is for any other intimate, loving relationship.

However, although love is, along with obedience, commitment, and service, repeatedly taught as being the cornerstone of relationship with

---

2. Martin, *Between Heaven and Mirth*, loc. 3941.

God the possibility of laughing together and sharing a sense of humor is less often—rarely—seen as important. Psychologists are more likely to see the importance of laughter for marital relationships than theologians are to see it as being significant in one's relationship with God. Business consultants are more likely to stress the role of laughter than spiritual advisors. Yet it is clear that satisfaction with the relationship, the stability of the relationship, and levels of commitment are all enhanced by laughter. But when considering this in regard to one's relationship with God it is important to recognize that laughter itself is not something one just imports or cultivates in order to achieve these ends (even though they are good goals to seek and even despite the fact that laughter does achieve them), because laughter is not so much a utilitarian tool to be employed in a relationship as simply an expression of the relationship itself—a genuine, unmistakable sign of joy and faith. Laughter is an intrinsic part of one's relationship with God. In that sense, as a part of our relationship with God, laughter should be sought and enjoyed as a good in itself (rather than as a means to an end). It is something that God wants to share in with us as a part of a relationship of love. God loves to laugh.

The relationship between laughter and love is the most important connection that needs to be made but in a logical sense it is not the first. Prior to this is the role that humor plays in *the human awareness of transcendence and in the acknowledgement of God*. The one who turns to God may do so as the result of an experience of the magnificence of the world and the majesty of God the Creator, or with a new awareness of sin and thus of the salvation of God the Redeemer, but whether awe or repentance is dominant the comic is also needed, even if its role is not well understood. Reinhold Niebuhr wrote that "humor is a proof of the capacity of the self to gain a vantage point from which it is able to look at itself. The sense of humor is thus a by-product of self-transcendence."[3] The human person is a complex entity, both wonderfully made and amazingly flawed, both beautiful and tragic. Comprehending both of these dimensions is important for self-understanding, and yet even doing that is inadequate for they both tend to take the person so seriously when there is also a certain comic absurdity about both our failings and our successes. This comes to the fore at the moment that there is a recognition that there is one who stands outside, beyond and above us—an Other who is ready to forgive our failings and who desires to show us successes beyond our imagination.

3. Niebuhr, *Essential*, 54.

No tallying of either failings or successes can establish who we are, and it is necessary—with apologies to Rudyard Kipling for this reinterpretation of his poem—to "treat those two impostors just the same," not just to become "a man,"[4] but to be able to overcome our own narrow self-assessment and to be graced with a completely different perspective on life lived *coram deo* (in the presence of God). Karl Rahner advises,

> Laugh. For this laughter is an acknowledgement that you are a human being, an acknowledgement that is itself the beginning of an acknowledgement of God. For how else is a person to acknowledge God except through admitting in his life and by means of his life that he himself is not God but a creature that has his times—a time to weep and a time to laugh, and the one is not the other. A praising of God is what laughter is, because it lets the human being be human.[5]

An inability to recognize one's own, very human limitations in comparison to God's limitless, but unfathomable, authority is simply the result of pride, an inappropriate estimation of one's own worth and position in the universe. Turning away from this to a recognition of one's true humanity and God's true divinity is the beginning of the road to salvation. An awareness of the proper form of relationship between God and humanity is worthy of laughter. As it has been said, "If you want to make God laugh, tell him about your plans." And anyone can join in this laughter when they come to recognize the truth of it.

Truth and humor

This awareness of the difference, the incongruity, between the human and the divine is but the beginning of an awareness of God and as this understanding grows humor continues to be an important tool in understanding and assessing truth. In this area at least, more than in others, the role of the comic has been philosophically well explored. The comic is important, thirdly, in the assessment of *the truth that is revealed through reason and logic* and fourthly, and even more importantly, in the closely related assessment of *the truth and wisdom that comes through the apparently irrational, the paradoxical and the foolish*. This role of the comic in revelation may

---

4. Kipling, *Works*, 605. "If you can meet with Triumph and Disaster/And treat those two impostors just the same . . . /you'll be a Man, my son!"

5. Cited in Martin, *Between Heaven and Mirth*, loc. 3397.

THE COMIC CHRISTIAN LIFE

be seen as it developed in the closely related writings of three philosophers of the comic. The first is Anthony Ashley Cooper, the third Earl of Shaftesbury (1671–1713), who wrote about the role of humor in reason; the second is the Lutheran Johann Georg Hamann (1730–1788), who was much influenced by Shaftesbury and developed the connection between humor and reason to include the significance of paradox. He, in turn, was a profound influence on Søren Kierkegaard (1813–1885), who regarded Hamann as "the greatest humorist in Christianity."[6] Hamann, however, is not widely known, something that is also true of the theology of humor generally, and it was Kierkegaard who built on Hamann's understanding of humor and made the philosophy of humor more accessible. And he made it possible for some Christian thinkers of the twentieth century, such as Reinhold Niebuhr, to develop an interest in it. Shaftesbury undertook the first extensive examination of the use of various forms of humor, especially ridicule but also wit and good humor, as important epistemological tools that promote truth and rationality.[7] He argued that ridicule is a basic test of truth. Any statement that is able to be ridiculed and that thus has an underlying incongruity is untrue. Secondly, he argued (with Aristotle) that the openness which good humor produces is an essential part of the search for truth as well as an effect and evidence of rationality.

Humor, therefore, has an important role in the assessment of truth and this, incidentally, has significant implications for free speech. In a reasonable society all things, even God, should potentially be exposed to ridicule for in the end only that which is deformed or inconsistent or unreasonable can really be affected by ridicule. That which is good and reasonable will not be hurt by it; the reasonable will always endure. And so, because ridicule will only hurt that which is false it should be allowed and, as such, it can serve society well by being the means of discrediting faulty and fanatical notions of God and truth.

In this way Shaftesbury clarified the connection between humor and truth but his logical and ethically focused theology had little place for the paradoxical nature of Christ or the irrationality, the foolishness, of the gospel, unlike the philosophy of Johann Georg Hamann. Hamann, as noted above, was influenced by Shaftesbury in regard to the connection between

---

6. Amir, *Humor and the Good Life*, 99.

7. According to Alfred O. Aldridge, it was his followers, rather than Shaftesbury himself, who made his comments on ridicule a fundamental test of truth. See Aldridge, "Shaftesbury and the Test of Truth," 129–56.

humor and truth, but for Hamann Christ was central and so his thought also deals with the inherent paradox of Christ as well as "the infinite incongruity between man and God."[8] For Hamann, humor, which is the only real way to grasp incongruity, is *the* way to comprehend the paradoxical truth about God. This laughter is not the same as the laughter that comes from the ridicule that exposes false and unreasonable claims to truth. Ridicule that exposes the truth is funny but not always joyful because that which is ridiculed may well have involved people in some form of injustice or suffering or oppression. There is thus a tendency for it to elicit ambivalent feelings, laughter at those exposed as foolish or unreasonable, and empathy for those who have been victims of it. On the other hand, the laughter that comes from a recognition of what God has done in the incarnation and in the salvation of the world is truly joyful and wonderful. In the face of these truths there is rejoicing at the grace and the love of God and at the gift of salvation that has been provided.

In Kierkegaard's way of thinking, having an "ethic of the comic" is essential. The "religious" is the purest philosophy of life (above the ethical and the aesthetic, as noted in chapter 8) and the religious person is the one who has discovered the comic on the greatest scale and "the more competently a person exists, the more he will discover the comic" including the contradictions (or incongruities) that the comic necessarily involves.[9] This does not mean that the religious person is a joker, a trickster, or a buffoon: the one who has a comic view of life is not necessarily the person who tells more jokes. But they do have a different, particular view of life, and relationship with God and others. Those without a genuine sense of humor will not fully understand themselves or the incongruities of the world or be able to discern the mystery, the wonder, the awesomeness of God. This is the foolishness of the gospel that defies human wisdom. It is so because of the incarnation and the death of God in Christ that is at the heart of the Christian faith, and without all that is involved in a sense of humor one is completely unable to comprehend it.

Humanity cannot fully grasp the fundamentally incomprehensible, unknowable, unfathomable, mysterious truth of God and there are really only two appropriate responses to it. According to Parker J. Palmer they are a "spiritual odd-couple"; one is either silent in awe, or one laughs in joy.[10]

---

8. Amir, *Humor and the Good Life*, 92.
9. Kierkegaard, *Concluding Unscientific Postscript*, 462.
10. Palmer, "Laughter and Silence."

Silence is certainly appropriate as it stresses the inability of humanity to fathom the mind of God, but one cannot, I do not think, stay in that place forever! And one might well think that laughter is more a more positive, accepting, and affirming response that rejoices in the greatness of God! This is not merely a case of laughing "with" God, but a genuine case of laughing "at" God, the one who has turned the tables on everyone and done the logically unimaginable, the wonderfully unexpected, and the graciously unwarranted. And the point is that this paradoxical truth is only accessible to those with a sense of humor. It is not comprehended by logic or understood by reason. It can only be accepted joyfully and laughingly by faith as an act of grace. Humor is thus an essential part of the reception of the *revelation* of God and, as much as is possible, the means of the comprehension of the paradoxical, incongruous truth of Jesus Christ.

Humor, humility, and holiness

One of the greatest attributes of the paradoxical God is that divine humility that enables God to become incarnate and suffer death. This humility is an essential correlate of divine grace. It is an inner attitude of sacrifice towards self that complements the passion to give lavishly to others. As obverse and reverse are sides to one coin so are humility and grace to the character of God. In humanity the presence of humility and the reception of grace are also connected, though in a somewhat different manner. In God there is no "before" and "after" but in the human context one can say that humility comes before grace. Humility is an essential precondition for being able to receive the divine grace that is offered for, as the epistle of James says, "God resists the proud, but gives grace to the humble" (4:6). Consequently, the attribute that it is most necessary as one comes to God is humility. The one who does not understand the need for it cannot comprehend God or the gospel. But although we have noted that grace is, like with a coin, the obverse of humility, the analogy now suddenly needs to consider the possibility of a three-sided coin for in a different sense the other side of humility is humor! True humility involves the ability to not only repent of one's frailties and failures in the light of God's law, but also to be confident enough to laugh at them in the light of God's grace. Humility without a strong sense of the corresponding grace of God leads to self-condemnation rather than to laughter. Humility—and that means humor—is necessary in order to understand one's place before God. Humor is essential for humility and the apprehension of God, of divine foolishness, and of the paradoxical truth of incarnation and salvation. And so humility with humor is the way to repentance, and because it is more than a single act, but rather the beginning of a new way of life, *humor is the way to a life of holiness*. This relationship between *humor, humility, and holiness* is the fifth connection to be drawn between the laughter and salvation. Etymologically the "saints" (from the Latin *sanctus*, which is a translation of the Greek *hagios*, meaning "holy") are those who are holy and so it is perhaps a pity that St. Philip Neri (1515–95) alone is known as "the humorous saint," for this is a characteristic that should be more widely associated with the people of God. To be holy is to be set apart as belonging to God and reflecting the divine character. This does not mean undertaking a perpetually serious or somber state of being; rather it is a way of life that should be more characterized by joy and laughter. Laughter is an expression of one's relationship with God, a part of that holiness without which one cannot see God (Heb 12:14). It is humor and laughter that express a fundamental humility about oneself and the world, which reveals the paradoxical truth about the foolishness of God in Christ Jesus, and which are expressions of faith in God and joy at the resurrection. A sense of humor is therefore, one might say, an essential of the Christian way of life in terms of both the revelation of, and the relationship with, God.

Sixthly, growth in holiness also takes place because of the connection between *humor and the creative imagination*. Anita Houck notes that "humour can contribute to the religious imagination, and thus to holiness, by challenging established images of the holy, inviting fresh theological reflection, and inspiring ethical action. Both holiness and humour require openness to that which is beyond us and agility in responding to the other."[11] An imagination that utilizes humor opens itself to multilayered and complex interactions in a very relational manner. It is possible to use humor to challenge inadequate images of God, to provoke thought about commonplace images and ideas and to speculate about possibilities. It has often been noted that the use of humor in brainstorming increases the level of creativity, breaks out of established ways of thinking, and blocks negative emotions. The ancient practice of *risus paschalis* was one means by which the church gave permission and encouragement to the utilization of humor. Today, in the absence of any liturgical support, one finds the main support for it in Christian writing. However, most Christian literature that utilizes humor in

---

11. Houck, "Holiness and Humour," 1.

the exploration of the character of God, the nature of the church, or the form of the Christian life is not seen as terribly "serious." In one sense that is inevitable, because it is not, but frivolity ought not be automatically confused with a lack of serious intent. A few writers have achieved significant recognition for their work in this regard, including C. S. Lewis for *The Screwtape Letters*, which illuminates the nature of both good and evil, and G. K. Chesterton in his numerous radio broadcasts, newspaper articles, and books.

The comic and community

An obvious but important seventh point to note as we come to the end of this study of laughter is that *humor is fundamentally a communal activity*. It has repeatedly been shown that people are more likely to laugh at something funny when they are with others than when they are by themselves. Humor is particularly appreciated in the company of friends, though the presence of others who are not so close also encourages laughter. Humor is both the result of friendship and a generator of it, and a shared sense of humor demonstrates a level of intimacy and understanding between people. It creates trust and a sense of togetherness. It affirms group identity and group solidarity. This is all true for virtually any group of people, but it is especially true that there is a connection between humor and the life of the Christian community. What is important for the Christian community is not so much telling jokes or buffoonery as exhibiting a lightness of being about life, ministry, and faith. It is in regard to the development of holiness that it is important to create, or recover, a certain level of levity within the community of believers. In doing this the life of the community will be enhanced.

It has been strongly argued through this book that the utilitarian benefits of laughter, although significant, are not themselves the primary reason for a theological and spiritual recognition of the role of humor. Nonetheless, although utility is not the main thing, humor does have important social and psychological side benefits (although the connection between humor and well-being is more complex than often assumed—not all the positive effects that are claimed are proven and there may be some negative effects as well).[12] There is, however, a healthy, clear, and positive relationship between humor and hope and thus, eighthly, *a positive correlation between humor and overcoming melancholy, depression, despair, and anger*. To have

---

12. Collicutt and Gray, "A Merry Heart Doeth Good Like a Medicine."

a sense of humor in the midst of difficulty, suffering, or even tragedy is to be hopeful. The language used reflects one's fundamental attitude towards the dilemmas of life, as when people are commonly described as "battling" cancer. This is undoubtedly one appropriate approach but it ought not be seen as negating the possibility of other metaphors and attitudes so that one does not necessarily "battle" with, or even simply "endure" or "live with" cancer, but perhaps one learns to "dance" with cancer, to "laugh" with Alzheimer's, and to "sing" in the presence of death. It is important to learn from those who have a spiritual sense of humor. Christians should practice laughing, which is to practice the presence of God.

The ninth theological connection between humor and the Christian way of life relates to the way in which humor influences both ministry and maturity. In short, the mature believer understands that a sense of humor is an essential part of Christian ministry. It is possible to be too serious as a Christian, which does not mean being less committed, but it does mean expressing more joy and laughter. Christians are to be childlike in their faith, which means sharing in the celebratory laughter that comes from an awareness of God and salvation and expressing the revolutionary humor of the gospel. *Humor is both an outcome of spiritual maturity and a means toward it.* It involves the ability to move beyond the self and see life through the eyes of God. Charles L. Campbell says,

> Ministry in the service of this free and living God will be characterized by open seriousness. Because ministry has to do with God, it is serious. And because it has to do with God, ministry remains open, for we cannot control God. Indeed, laughter may be the only way to engage seriously with the living God. God's Spirit continues to blow where she chooses (John 3:8), disrupting seriousness when it becomes closed, dogmatic, and idolatrous. The incarnate, crucified, resurrected Christ continues to work through the Spirit, interrupting, fracturing, cracking up in order to move people toward the fulfillment of God's purposes. Incarnation laughter, crucifixion laughter, and resurrection laughter are all expressions of the Spirit, who moves restlessly in the church and the world. Consequently, Christian ministry remains open to the disruptive surprises of the Spirit. Faithful Christian ministers laugh with open seriousness, welcoming life that is not complete, but is always "on the way," always living in the dynamic and fluid

movement between the old age that is dying and the new that continues to be born.[13]

The tenth and final point of connection between humor and the gospel of salvation is a reaffirmation of the true centrality of humor as an element of the Apostle Peter's declaration that "you may participate in the divine nature" (2 Pet 1:4). The comic dimension of the gospel is not merely an incidental extra, it is an intrinsically important aspect of it. This union is much more than being a member of a society, and there is no real correlate with any human relationship. It is the unique relationship a believer shares with Christ, a relationship of joy and laughter. It is this way because God *is* love and, as noted above, one cannot really love anyone with whom one never laughs. Altogether, biblical and theological humor is not merely episodic or incidental but fundamental and essential. There is a comic dimension to the gospel of salvation and to the nature of God.

The last laugh

This brings us back to the original purpose of this book, as expressed at the very beginning, that it is appropriate to have a theologically strong view of humor and laughter, where humor is closely related to central theological themes and has extensive implications for life and faith. The aim has been to show that humor is part of our relationship with God, an aspect of divine character, closely related to the central theological themes of incarnation, cross, and resurrection and an element of the apostle Peter's declaration that "you may participate in the divine nature" (2 Pet 1:4). Laughter is an essential part of a healthy spiritual life.

Can it therefore be said that God is a comic? This is a question that inevitably raises the issue of the well-known aphorism, "God is a comedian playing to an audience that is too afraid to laugh." This is a saying usually attributed to the French Enlightenment era satirical writer and philosopher François-Marie Arouet (1694–1778), better known by his pen name, Voltaire (an anagram of a Latin form of his name with connotations of speed and daring—as in volte-face, to turn abruptly—which certainly sounds more decisive and serious than his earlier nickname of Zozo). Voltaire declared himself to be a lover of God but was a great critic of the church and he used his considerable wit to ridicule what he saw as the absurdities of

13. Campbell, "Ministry with a Laugh," 206.

faith. Whether actually from Voltaire or not this saying can be interpreted in two ways. It can be taken as an expression, and perhaps a criticism, of the view that God is a comedian in the sense of being a capricious practical joker who needs to be feared. This is obviously not a view shared here. Alternatively the saying can be taken as suggesting that most people are simply too obtuse to understand the real nature of God's comic (and kind) character and thus are fearful of God when they ought to be laughing. Is Voltaire right to suggest that people actually been fearful of the humor of God when they ought to have been laughing? As we have seen in various parts of the discussion so far, that is absolutely the case. It is seen in changes made to one of the most continuously used hymns of the past 500 years. Some hymnals of the late nineteenth and twentieth century modified William Kethe's hymn "All people that on earth do well," allowing the second line "Sing to the Lord with cheerful voice" to stand, but changing the next line, "Him serve with *mirth*, his praise forth tell" to the apparently more theologically acceptable, "him serve with *fear*, his praise forth tell." It appears, for example, in this form in the Harvard Classics compilation of *Hymns of the Christian Church* published in 1909–14. The term *mirth* is not used as much today as it was in the past when it was commonly used to express laughter, merriment, and joviality. Kethe was right to see it as accurately reflecting the joyfulness of the original psalm ("Worship the LORD with gladness; come before him with joyful songs . . . Enter his gates with thanksgiving and his courts with praise; For the LORD is good and his love endures forever.").

The rejection of mirth in favor of fear is a tragic reflection on the attitude of the church to God's sense of humor. It has the effect of making it hard for people to accept the notion of God being a comic or comedian but in reality God does not merely have a sense of humor that responds to the humor that others produce, God is the creator of humor as much as of any other part of the created world, and it reflects the divine character. One who actively creates humor is a comic but not the wisecracking and often annoying kind of comic for whom everything is a joke, the kind of person who is perpetually trivializing the important. Even less is God the kind of comedian who is capricious and always having a joke at someone else's expense. An all-powerful God like that would indeed need to be feared. God is a comic who is a friend who has a love of laughter. Humor expresses God's complete love for the world and it undercuts any notion of God as an authoritarian, humorless controller of all things. God is a comedian or comic in the sense of one who loves to interact with others in very personal and delightful, joyful ways. God calls on us to participate in a life of love and laughter. God *is* genuinely a comedian who has the last laugh. Nobody laughs like God does.

In the Christian life there is not only a time to weep but also definitely a time to laugh (Eccl 3:4), because the Bible is fundamentally, in the classical sense, a divine comedy that ends with joy and laughter. And the running joke throughout is that God appears in the most unexpected, the least likely places, as when born to a poor, young, unmarried virgin in an obscure and occupied country. The idea of God incarnate, as part of his own creation, and of the incarnate Christ dying at the hands of people created by God is truly absurd, a radical, genuine scandal. It is very appropriate that it should produce laughter in everyone who hears of it, though people will laugh in different ways. Those who are not believers are within their rights to laugh in derision and mockery because, after all, the notion of the Lord of the universe requiring nappies, and the idea of Son of God dying on a cross, are foolishness according to any purely human form of reckoning. Those who are believers also laugh, but their laughter is very different, for they laugh genuinely and joyfully. Ironically, until one has seen the humor in what God has done one has not yet taken it seriously enough. This laughter of the faithful is nothing other than the sound of joy that comes as a gift from God. Bildad, the friend of Job, said some foolish things but he got it right when he said, "He will yet fill your mouth with laughter and your lips with shouts of joy" (Job 8:21) and this is what God will do for all. Love and laughter go together hand in hand. We love those who make us laugh and we laugh with those we love. There can be no real love without laughter. The importance of laughter in a relationship is not adequately measured by the amount of time one actually spends laughing. Laughter is indicative of the fundamental nature of the relationship. It both reveals and creates the bonds of love and friendship that exist. There is no doubt that laughter should be very much a part of everyone's spiritual life for in it one participates in the life, the love and the laughter of God. It is not only Sarah, but every believer that can say, "God has brought me laughter, and everyone who hears about this will laugh with me" (Gen 21:6).

Bibliography

Alcorn, Randy C. *Happiness*. Carol Stream, IL: Tyndale House, 2015.
Aldridge, Owen. "Shaftesbury and the Test of Truth." *PMLA* 60 (1945) 129–56.
Amir, Lydia. *Humor and the Good Life in Modern Philosophy: Shaftesbury, Hamann, Kierkegaard*. Albany, NY: State University of New York Press, 2014.
Andronovienė, Lina. "The Practice of Humour and Our Spirituality: Some Reflections." *Journal of European Baptist Studies* 14, no. 3 (May 2014) 22–33.
Apte, Mahadev L. *Humor and Laughter: An Anthropological Approach*. Ithaca, NY: Cornell University Press, 1985.
Aquinas, Thomas. *The Summa Theologica*. Translated by English Dominicans. Chicago: Encyclopaedia Britannica, 1955.
Aristotle. *The Rhetoric and the Poetics of Aristotle*. New York: Random House, 1954.
———. *Nichomachean Ethics*. Translated by J. A. K. Thomson. London: Penguin, 2004.
Athanasius of Alexandria. *On the Incarnation*. England: Pantianos Classics, 1944.
Attardo, Salvatore. *Encyclopedia of Humor Studies*. Los Angeles: SAGE Reference, 2014.
Bain, Alexander. *The Emotions and the Will*. London: J. W. Parker, 1859.
Barth, Karl. *The Church Dogmatics*. Vol. IV/3. Edinburgh: T & T Clark, 1961.
———. *Evangelical Theology: An Introduction*. Grand Rapids: Eerdmans, 1963
Basil of Caesarea. "On the Perfection of Solitaries." In *A Select Library of the Nicene and Post-Nicene Fathers*, vol. VIII, edited by Philip Schaff and Henry Wace, 127–9. Grand Rapids: Eerdmans, 1978.
Bednarz, Terri. *Humor in the Gospels: A Sourcebook for the Study of Humor in the New Testament 1863–2014*. New York: Lexington, 2015.
Benatar, David. "Taking Humour (Ethics) Seriously, But Not Too Seriously." *Journal of Practical Ethics* 2, no. 1 (2014) 24–43.
Benedict of Nursia. *The Rule of St. Benedict*. London: SPCK, 1931.
Berg, William, ed. and trans. *Philologos: the Laugh Addict*. London: Yudu Media, 2008. Accessed at www.yudu.org.
Berger, Peter L. *Redeeming Laughter: The Comic Dimension of Human Experience*. Berlin: Walter de Gruyter, 2014.
Bergson, Henri. "Laughter." In *Comedy*, edited by Wylie Sypher, 59–190. Garden City, NY: Doubleday, 1956.
Bessière, Gérard. "Humour—a Theological Attitude." In *Theology of Joy*, 81–95. New York: Herder and Herder, 1974.

Billig, Michael. *Laughing and Ridicule: Towards a Social Critique of Laughter.* London: Sage, 2005.
Bingham, Shawn Chandler, and Sara E. Green. *Seriously Funny: Disability and the Paradoxical Power of Humor.* Boulder, CO: Lynne Rienner, 2016.
Bowen, Barbara C. *Humor and Humanism in the Renaissance.* Aldershot: Ashgate, 2004.
Brenner, Athalya, and Yehuda Thomas Radday. *On Humour and the Comic in the Hebrew Bible.* Bible and Literature Series. Sheffield, England: Sheffield Academic, 1990.
Campbell, Charles L. "Ministry with a Laugh." *Interpretation* 69, no. 2 (April 2015) 196–208.
Capper, John. "Karl Barth's Theology of Joy." PhD thesis, Cambridge University, 1998.
Capps, Donald. "Gossip, Humor, and the Art of Becoming an Intimate of Jesus." *Journal of Religion & Health* 51, no. 1 (March 2012) 99–117.
———. *A Time to Laugh: The Religion of Humor.* New York: Continuum, 2005.
Carrell, Amy. "Historical Views of Humor." In *The Primer of Humor Research*, edited by Victor Raskin, 303–30. Berlin: Mouton de Gruyter, 2008.
Carroll, Noël. *Humour: A Very Short Introduction.* Oxford: Oxford University Press, 2014.
Carter, Judy. *The Comedy Bible: From Stand-up to Sitcom—the Comedy Writer's Ultimate "How To" Guide.* New York: Simon and Shuster, 2001.
Chafe, Wallace. *The Importance of Not Being Earnest: The Feeling behind Laughter and Humor.* Amsterdam: John Benjamins, 2007.
Chapman, Antony J., and Hugh C Foot. *Humour and Laughter: Theory, Research, and Applications.* London: John Wiley and Sons, 1976.
Charney, Maurice. *Comedy: A Geographic and Historical Guide.* Westport, CT: Praeger, 2005.
Chesterton, G. K. *Lunacy and Letters.* New York: Sheed and Ward, 1958.
Choate, Pearson. *The Laughing Christ.* Sydney: Angus and Robertson, 1933.
Christian, Graham. "God Laughed." *Library Journal* 139, no. 9 (May 15, 2014) 62.
Chrysostom, John. "Homilies on the Gospel of St Matthew." In *A Select Library of the Nicene and Post-Nicene Fathers*, vol. X, edited by Philip Schaff, 1–536. Grand Rapids: Eerdmans, 1978.
Claassens, L. Juliana. "Tragic Laughter: Laughter as Resistance in the Book of Job." *Interpretation* 69, no. 2 (April 2015) 143–55.
Classen, Albrecht. *Laughter in the Middle Ages and Early Modern Times: Epistemology of a Fundamental Human Behavior, Its Meaning, and Consequences.* Berlin: De Gruyter, 2010.
Clement of Alexandria. "Paedogogus." In *Ante-Nicene Fathers*, vol. 2, edited by Alexander Roberts, James Donaldson, and A. Cleveland Coxe, 207–98. Grand Rapids: Eerdmans, 1979.
Cohen, Ted. *Jokes: Philosophical Thoughts on Joking Matters.* Chicago: University of Chicago Press, 1999.
Collicutt, Joanna, and Amanda Gray. "A Merry Heart Doeth Good like a Medicine: Humour, Religion and Wellbeing." *Mental Health, Religion and Culture* 15, no. 8 (October 2012) 759–78.
Conolly, Oliver, and Bashshar Haydar. "The Good, the Bad and the Funny." *Monist* 88, no. 1 (January 2005) 121–34.
Cooper, Anthony Ashley. *Characteristicks of Men, Manners, Opinions, Time.* Vol. 1. Edited by Douglas Den Uyl. Indianapolis: Liberty Fund, 2001. http://oll.libertyfund.org/titles/811.

Critchley, Simon. *On Humour.* London: Routledge, 2002.
Davies, Christie. *Jokes and Their Relation to Society.* Berlin: Mouton de Gruyter, 1998.
Davies, Stephanie. *Laughology: Improve Your Life with the Science of Laughter.* Carmarthen, Wales: Crown House, 2013.
Davis, Murray S. *What's so Funny? The Comic Conception of Culture and Society.* Chicago: University of Chicago Press, 1993.
De Sousa, Ronald. *The Rationality of Emotion.* Cambridge, MA: MIT Press, 1987.
Donnelly, Doris. "Divine Folly: Being Religious and the Exercise of Humor." *Theology Today* 48, no. 4 (January 1992) 385–96.
Downey, Patrick. *The Philosophical and Theological Significance of Tragic and Comic Writing in the Western Tradition.* Lanham, MD: Lexington, 2001.
Dunn, Joseph R. *Psychological and Biblical Perspectives on Humor.* Jackson, MS: American Association of Christian Counselors, 1987.
Dunne, Michael. *Calvinist Humor in American Literature.* Baton Rouge, LA: Louisiana State University Press, 2007.
Durant, John, and Jonathan Miller. *Laughing Matters: A Serious Look at Humour.* Harlow, UK: Longman Scientific and Technical, 1988.
Eagleton, Terry. *The Meaning of Life: A Very Short Introduction.* Oxford: Oxford University Press, 2007.
Eckardt, A. Roy. *How to Tell God from the Devil: On the Way to Comedy.* New Brunswick, NJ: Transaction, 1995.
Edgar, Brian. *God Is Friendship: A Theology of Spirituality, Community and Society.* Wilmore, KY: Seedbed, 2013.
———. *The God Who Plays: A Playful Approach to Theology and Spirituality.* Eugene, OR: Cascade, 2017.
Evans, Robert John Weston. *The Humour of History and the History of Humour.* Oxford: Dacre Trust, 2012.
Figueroa Dorrego, Jorge, ed. *A Source Book of Literary and Philosophical Writings about Humour and Laughter: The Seventy-Five Essential Texts from Antiquity to Modern Times.* Lewiston, NY: Edwin Mellen, 2009.
Fitzhenry, Robert, ed. *The Harper Book of Quotations.* 3rd edition. New York: HarperCollins, 1993.
Freud, Sigmund. *The Joke and Its Relation to the Unconscious.* Translated by Joyce Crick, with an Introduction by John Carey. London: Penguin, 2002.
Goatly, Andrew. *Meaning and Humour.* Cambridge: Cambridge University Press, 2012.
Goldstein, Jeffrey H. *The Psychology of Humor: Theoretical Perspectives and Empirical Issues.* New York: Academic, 1972.
Grassi, Joseph A. *God Makes Me Laugh: A New Approach to Luke.* Eugene, OR: Wipf and Stock, 2009.
Gregory of Nyssa. "The Great Catechism." In *A Select Library of the Nicene and Post-Nicene Fathers,* second series, vol. V, edited by Philip Schaff and Henry Wace, 471–509. Grand Rapids: Eerdmans, 1979.
Gutwirth, Marcel. *Laughing Matter: An Essay on the Comic.* Ithaca, NY: Cornell University Press, 1993.
Hafiz, and Daniel Ladinsky. *I Heard God Laughing: Poems of Hope and Joy: Renderings of Hafiz.* New York: Penguin, 2006.
Hazlitt, William. *Lectures on English Comic Writers.* Oxford: Oxford University Press, 1907.

Heddendorf, Russell. *From Faith to Fun: The Secularisation of Humour.* Cambridge: Lutterworth, 2009.
Hegel, Georg W. F. *The Philosophy of Fine Art.* Vol. 4. London: G. Bell, 1920.
Hobbes, Thomas. "Human Nature." In *The English Works of Thomas Hobbes*, 4:1–76. London: John Bohn, 1840.
Holweck, F. "Easter." In *The Catholic Encyclopedia.* New York: Robert Appleton Company, 1909. http://www.newadvent.org/cathen/05224d.htm.
Houck, Anita. "Holiness and Humour." *HTS Teologiese Studies* 72, no. 4 (2016) 1–8.
Huizinga, Johan. *Homo Ludens: A Study of the Play Element in Culture.* Boston: Beacon, 1955.
Hyers, M. Conrad. *And God Created Laughter: The Bible as Divine Comedy.* Atlanta: John Knox, 1987.
———. *The Comic Vision and the Christian Faith: A Celebration of Life and Laughter.* New York: Pilgrim, 1981.
———. *Holy Laughter: Essays on Religion in the Comic Perspective.* New York: Seabury, 1969.
Insella, John, ed. *The Penguin Anthology of Australian Poetry.* Melbourne: Penguin, 2008.
Iverson, Kelly R. "Incongruity, Humor, and Mark: Performance and the Use of Laughter in the Second Gospel (Mark 8.14–21)." *New Testament Studies* 59, no. 1 (January 2013) 2–19.
Jonson, Ben. *Every Man in His Humour.* Edited by Robert Miola. Manchester: Manchester University Press, 2008.
———. *Every Man Out of His Humour.* Edited by Helen Ostovich. Manchester: Manchester University Press, 2001.
Jónsson, Jakob. *Humor and Irony in the New Testament: Illuminated by Parallels in Talmud and Midrash.* Leiden: Brill, 1985.
Joubert, Laurent. *Treatise On Laughter.* Translated by Gregory de Rocher. Tuscaloosa, AL: The University of Alabama, 1980
Kaminsky, Joel S. "Humor and the Theology of Hope: Isaac as a Humorous Figure." *Interpretation* 54, no. 4 (October 2000) 363–75.
Kant, Immanuel. *Critique of Judgement.* Translated by J. C. Meredith. Oxford: Oxford University Press. 1911.
Keener, Craig. *The IVP Bible Background Commentary: New Testament.* 2d ed. Downers Grove, IL: IVP Academic, 2014.
Kierkegaard, Søren. *Concluding Unscientific Postscript to Philosophical Fragments.* Vol 1. Edited and translated by Howard V. Hong and Edna H. Hong. Princeton, NJ: Princeton University Press, 1941.
Kipling, Rudyard. *The Works of Rudyard Kipling.* Ware, Hertfordshire: Wordsworth Editions, 1994.
Koehler, Ed. *Amusing Grace.* Downers Grove, IL: InterVarsity, 1988.
Krosney, Herbert. *The Lost Gospel: The Quest for the Gospel of Judas Iscariot.* Washington, DC: National Geographic Society, 2007.
Kuschel, Karl-Josef. *Laughter: A Theological Essay.* London: SCM, 1994.
Latré, Guido. *Risus Mediaevalis: Laughter in Medieval Literature and Art.* Leuven: Leuven University Press, 2003.
Lewis, Clive Staples. *The Screwtape Letters.* London: Geoffrey Bles, 1942.
Longenecker, Bruce. "A Humorous Jesus? Orality, Structure and Characterisation in Luke 14:15–24, and Beyond." *Biblical Interpretation* 16, no. 2 (April 2008) 179–204.

BIBLIOGRAPHY

Lorenz, Konrad. *On Aggression*. 3rd edition. Abingdon: Routledge Classics, 2002.
Ludovici, Anthony. *The Secret of Laughter*. London: Constable, 1932
McClintock, John, and James Strong, eds. "Lentulus." In the *Cyclopaedia of Biblical, Theological, and Ecclesiastical Literature*, vol. 5, 348–51. New York: Harper, 1880.
Manser, Martin, compiler. *The Westminster Collection of Christian Quotations*. London: Westminster John Knox, 2001.
Martin, James. *Between Heaven and Mirth: Why Joy, Humor and Laughter are at the Heart of the Spiritual Life*. Kindle ed. New York: Harper One, 2011.
———. "Rejoice Always!" *America* 205, no. 9 (October 3, 2011) 12–16.
Moltmann, Jürgen. *Theology and Joy*. London: SCM, 1973.
———. *Theology of Play*. New York: Harper & Row, 1972.
Morreall, John. *Comedy, Tragedy, and Religion*. Albany, NY: State University of New York, 1999.
———. *Comic Relief: A Comprehensive Philosophy of Humor*. Chichester: Wiley-Blackwell, 2009.
———. "Philosophy and Religion." In *The Primer of Humor Research*, edited by Victor Raskin, 211–42. Berlin: De Gruyter Mouton, 2008.
———. "Philosophy of Humor." In the *Stanford Encyclopedia of Philosophy* (Winter 2016 edition). Edited by Edward N. Zalta. https://plato.stanford.edu/archives/win2016/entries.humor/.
———. *Philosophy of Humor and Laughter*. Albany, NY: State University of New York, 1987.
Morton, Russell. "Acts 12:1–19." *Interpretation* 55, no. 1 (January 2001) 67–69.
Murray, David P. "Serious Preaching in a Comedy Culture." *Puritan Reformed Journal* 3, no. 1 (January 2011) 328–38.
Niebuhr, Reinhold. *Discerning the Signs of the Times: Sermons for Today and Tomorrow*. New York: Charles Scribner's Sons, 1946.
———. *The Essential Reinhold Niebuhr: Selected Essays and Addresses*. Edited by Robert McAfee Brown. New Haven, CT: Yale University Press, 1986.
Nietzsche, Friedrich. *Thus Spake Zarathustra*. Translated by Thomas Common. Edinburgh: T. N. Foulis, 1909.
Norrick, Neal R. *Conversational Joking: Humor in Everyday Talk*. Bloomington, IN: Indiana University Press, 1993.
Oden, Thomas. *The Humor of Kierkegaard: An Anthology*. Princeton, NJ: Princeton University Press, 2004.
Ostrower, Chaya. "Humor as a Defense Mechanism during the Holocaust." *Interpretation* 69, no. 2 (April 2015) 183–95.
Palmer, Jerry. *Taking Humour Seriously*. London: Routledge, 1994.
Palmer, Parker J. "Laughter and Silence: The Spiritual Odd Couple." *On Being*. https://onbeing.org/blog/laughter-silence-the-spiritual-odd-couple/.
Palmer, Earl. F. *The Humor of Jesus: Sources of Laughter in the Bible*. Vancouver, BC: Regent College, 2001.
Parkin, John. *Humour Theorists of the Twentieth Century*. Lampeter, Wales: Edwin Mellen, 1997.
Patella, Michael. "And God Created Laughter: The Eighth Day." *Interpretation* 69, no. 2 (April 2015) 156–68.
Pelham, Abigail. "Job as Comedy, Revisited." *Journal for the Study of the Old Testament* 35, no. 1 (September 2010) 89–112.

Plato. *Philebus*. Translated by J. C. B. Gosling. Oxford: Clarendon, 1975.
Price, Lucien. *Dialogues of Alfred North Whitehead*. New York: New American Library, 1956.
Radday, Yehuda Thomas, and Brenner Athalya. *On Humour and the Comic in the Hebrew Bible*. Sheffield, England: Almond, 1990.
Rahner, Hugo. *Man at Play, Or, Did You Ever Practise Eutrapelia?* London: Burns & Oates, 1965.
Rahner, Karl. *The Content of Faith: The Best of Karl Rahner's Theological Writings*. New York: Crossroad, 1993.
Ramm, Bernard. "The Laughing Barth." In *After Fundamentalism: The Future of Evangelical Theology*, 193–97. San Francisco: Harper and Row, 1983.
Roeckelein, Jon E. *The Psychology of Humor: A Reference Guide and Annotated Bibliography*. Westport, CT: Greenwood, 2002.
Samra, Cal. *The Joyful Christ: The Healing Power of Humor*. San Francisco: Harper and Row, 1986.
Sands, Kathleen M. "Ifs, Ands, and Butts: Theological Reflections on Humor." *Journal of the American Academy of Religion* 64, no. 3 (September 1996) 499–523.
Sayers, Dorothy. *The Man Born to be King: A Play Cycle on the Life of our Lord and Saviour Jesus Christ*. Eugene, OR: Wipf and Stock, 2011.
Schleiermacher, Friedrich. *The Christian Faith*. Edited by H. R. Mackintosh and J. S. Stewart. Edinburgh: T and T Clark, 1986.
Schmidt-Clausing, Fritz. *The Humor of Huldrych Zwingli: The Lighter Side of the Protestant Reformation*. Edited and translated by Jim West. Lewiston, NY: Edwin Mellen, 2007.
Schneemelcher, Wilhelm. *New Testament Apocrypha*. Vol. 2. Rev. ed. Cambridge: James Clarke, 1992.
Schopenhauer, Arthur. *The World as Will and Idea*. Translated by R. B. Haldane and J. Kemp. London: Routledge and Kegan Paul, 1950.
Screech, Michael A. *Laughter at the Foot of the Cross*. Boulder, CO: Westview, 1999.
Sharpe, Robert A. "Seven Reasons Why Amusement is an Emotion." *Journal of Value Inquiry* 9 (1975) 201–3.
Strange, Marcian. "God and Laughter." *Worship* 45, no. 1 (n.d.) 1–12.
Torrance, Thomas F. *Karl Barth: Biblical and Evangelical Theologian*. Edinburgh: T and T Clark, 1990.
Torretta, Gabriel. "Preaching on Laughter: The Theology of Laughter in Augustine's Sermons." *Theological Studies* 76, no. 4 (December 2015) 742–64.
Trueblood, Elton. *The Humor of Christ*. San Francisco: HarperSanFrancisco, 1990.
Twain, Mark. *Following The Equator*. New York: Dover, 1989.
Vall, Gregory. "What Was Isaac Doing in the Field (Genesis XXIV 63)?" *Vetus Testamentum* 44, no. 4 (1994) 513–23.
Van Heerden, Willie. "Why the Humour in the Bible Plays Hide and Seek with Us." *Social Identities* 7, no. 1 (March 2001) 75–96.
Vogel, Heinrich. "Der lachende Barth." In *Antwort: Karl Barth zum Siebzigsten Gebürtstag*, edited by Ernst Wolf, Ch. Von Kirschbaum, and Rudolph Frey, 64–171. Zollikon-Zürich: Evangelischer Verlag, 1956.
Walker, Steven C. *Illuminating Humor of the Bible*. Eugene, OR: Cascade, 2013.
Wesley, Arun Kumar. "Mere Frivolity." *Asia Journal of Theology* 17, no. 1 (April 2003) 156–96.

Whedbee, J. William. *The Bible and the Comic Vision.* Cambridge: Cambridge University Press, 1998.
White, E. B., and Katharine White. *A Subtreasury of American Humor.* New York: Tudor, 1945.
Wilson, Christopher P. *Jokes: Form, Content, Use and Function.* London: Academic, 1979.
Witherington, Ben, III. *The Rest of Life: Rest, Play, Eating, Studying, Sex from a Kingdom Perspective.* Grand Rapids: Eerdmans, 2012.
Zuver, Dudley. *Salvation by Laughter: A Study of Religion and the Sense of Humor.* New York: Harper and Brothers, 1933.

Subject Index

absurd humor, 12
amusement, 6, 8–11, 17–18, 39
Aquinas, Thomas, *See* Thomas Aquinas.
Asbury Theological Seminary, x

Beatitudes, 37
Benedict, Rule of, ix, 73

Cana, wedding at, 35–36, 38, 47
cartoons, Danish, 70–71
Cavalier, the Laughing, 31
children, 37, 48, 54, 63–64, 74, 85, 100
Chinese humor, 13
Christ, the Laughing, 31
Comedia, 9
comedy, 9–11, 45–46, 57, 110, 121, 135
comical Biblical characters and situations, 42, 45–46
community, ix, 26, 32, 44, 124, 131–33
context, 12, 39, 69, 92
Confucian tradition, 13
covenant, 57–68
creativity, 130–31
cross and crucifixion, x, 5, 9, 27–28, 55, 103–6, 122, 133, 135
culture, 12–14, 24, 29–32, 54
cursing, 19

definitions of humor, 7–8
deification, 51, 86–87, 124
depression, 11, 124, 131–32
derision, 5, 40–1, 53, 135
discipleship, x
Divine Comedy, The, 9

Easter laugh, 100, 104–6
emotion, humor as, 14–15, 77, 89, 92–95
emotion, humor blocking, 14, 130
Essenes, 72
eutrapelia, 15, 101
Every Man in His Humor, 11
evil and the evil one, 108, 110–15, 121
explaining humor, 7–8

faith, laughter the language of, 7, 20–21, 48–56, 81 99–100, 129–34
family, 12–13
Fiddler on the Roof, 70
foolish characters, 39–42, 58, 103, 116
friendship, x, 12, 16, 92, 100–102, 135
fruit of the Spirit, 20

gender, 12–13, 29
God, humor and relationship with, 3, 21, 69–88, 123–24, 132–34
good, humor as a, 4–5, 20, 71–72, 78–79, 81–82, 125
Gospels, 28, 33–34, 36, 53–55,
grace, x, 2, 37, 50, 52, 64–65, 89–90, 98–102, 129

heaven, humor of, 10, 38, 41, 56, 69–88,
hoax, 30–31
holiness of humor, 81–85, 129–31
hope, 4, 20, 97, 109, 124, 131
humility, ix, 37, 42, 73, 129–31
humors, the ancient, 11
hyperbole, 35, 38, 41, 47, 49, 114

SUBJECT INDEX

imagination, 77, 124–25, 130–31
imago dei, 14
incarnation, x, 14, 55, 71, 84–87, 128–35
incongruity, 2, 9–10, 14–16, 18, 34, 43, 56, 72, 74, 76–77, 81–82, 85–87, 89–90, 94, 96–98, 101, 126–29
injustice, 5, 16, 44, 52–53, 56, 76, 87, 92, 107, 123, 128
innuendo, 38, 41
irony, 12, 15, 39, 50–52, 114–15, 118, 120–21
Islam, 71

jokes, 2, 5, 7–9, 12–13, 54, 70, 77–78, 95–96, 107, 134–35
joy, 3–4, 9–10, 15–16, 34–36, 41, 47, 53, 55–57, 64, 85–88, 106, 135
Judas, Gospel of, 27

lament, 108–110
Lazarus, 103–4
Lentulus, Epistle of, 26–27
Life of Brian, The, 70
love, x, 36, 84–86, 100, 124–26, 134–35

Magnificat, 17
Man Born to be King, The, 80
maturity, ix, 132
mockery, 16, 43–44, 103–4, 106–7
morality of humor, 5, 19–20, 71–72, 75–80

neuroscience, 95

offensive humor, 8, 13, 19, 71, 77–79
order of salvation, 123

Pachomius, Rule of, 72
parables, 18–19, 22–24, 30, 33, 38–42
paradox, 29, 34, 52–53, 60, 85, 87, 128
participation, in the life of God, 3–4, 87, 124, 133–24
pervasiveness of humor, 1–2
Peter, Apocalypse of, 27
Pharisees, 39–40, 43–44
physical aspects of humor, 11, 17, 106
play, x, 3–4, 90, 98–102

politics, 16–18, 71
prayer, 7, 21, 43

redeeming laughter, 87
relief theory of laughter, 89, 93–95
resurrection, x, 2, 106, 109
reversal, paradox and, 34, 52–53
risus paschalis, 105–6, 130

sanctification, x, 123
satan. *See* evil and the evil one.
satire, 1, 29, 33–34, 40, 50–52
Scripture, 24–26, 29, 57, 62, 105–6
self-deprecation, 1, 12, 93
sense of humor, 2, 12–16, 19–21, 25, 30, 34, 53, 56, 69–70, 79–86, 99, 124–5, 128–35
signals, of humor, 13
sin, 19–21, 74, 107, 115–20
slapstick, 1, 17
solemnity, 1, 3, 94
Song of Solomon, 60
spirituality, ix–x, 1–4, 72–75, 79, 90, 123–24, 132–35
subjective aspect of humor, 14–15, 30, 96
suffering, 5, 55, 60, 75, 79, 98, 103–122
superiority theory of humor, 15, 55, 76–78, 89–94

temperaments, 1–2, 14–16
theo-comical, 7
tragedy, x, 9–10, 16, 34, 45, 55, 57, 61–62, 109–110, 114–18, 118, 121–22
tragicomedy, 114
Trinity, x, 84–85, 99–100
truth, 4, 31, 39, 48, 89–90, 97, 118, 126–30

unconscious, the, 13, 95
universality, of humor, 14
Utopia, 18

virtue, 4, 19–21, 72
vision, Christian, 1, 123–35
vision, comic, 3, 10, 57–68, 123–35
vulnerability, 37

SUBJECT INDEX

weddings, 34, 36, 38–39, 47, 49, 56
wisdom, 4, 17–18, 34, 37, 57, 85, 117, 122, 126, 128
wit, 1–2, 13, 17, 22, 29, 93–94, 127, 133,
Woman, of Samaria, 35–36

Name Index

Abimelech, 66–67
Abraham, 62–66, 68, 74
Aelred of Rievaulx, 101
Amir, Lydia, 79, 82n19, 127n6, 128n8
Apte, Mahadev L., 13n8, 95
Aristotle, 15, 54, 76, 89, 91, 96, 101, 127
Augustine, 26, 74, 108

Bain, Alexander, 92
Barth, Karl, 89, 98–100, 108
Barton, Bruce, 80
Basil of Caesarea, 73–74
Beattie, James, 96
Bednarz, Terri, 28–29
Bergson, Henri, 92
Bessière, Gérard, 8
Brenner, Athalya, 26

Calvin, John, 99
Campbell, Charles L., vi, 132–33
Capps, Donald, 33n2, 81n17
Carter, Judy, 121
Chafe, Wallace, 15
Chesterton, G. K., 1, 3, 5, 131
Choate, Pearson, 31–32
Chrysostom, John, 73–74, 106
Cicero, 54
Clement of Alexandria, 73
Connolly, Oliver, 77
Cooper, Anthony Ashley, 94, 127
Curtius, Ernst Robert, 93

Descartes, René, 94
De Sousa, Ronald, 77

Donnelly, Doris, 123

Eagleton, Terry, 5–6, 97
Edgar, Brian, 35, 100–101
Elijah, 107
Ephraim the Syrian, 72
Esau, 66–67
Escher, M. C., 96
Esther, 57–58
Eusebius, 26

Freud, Sigmund, 13–14, 17, 94–5

Galen, 11, 94

Hals, Frans, 31
Hamann, Johann Georg, 127–28
Haydar, Bashshar, 77
Hazlitt, William, 92, 96–97
Hegel, Georg W. F., 91–92
Hierocles, 54
Hippocrates, 11
Hobbes, Thomas, 15, 76, 91, 93
Houck, Anita, 130
Huizinga, Johan, 4
Hutcheson, Francis, 93
Hyers, Conrad, 3, 81n17

Isaac, 35, 62–68
Isaiah, 58, 107

Jacob, 35, 67–68
James, brother of John, 45

NAME INDEX

Jesus, Christ, xi, 18–19, 22–57, 69–71, 75, 80–81, 100–101, 103–6, 112, 119, 122, 129–30
Job, 60, 110–22, 135
John the Baptist, 35–36, 81
Jonah, 58–60
Jonson, Ben, 11
Joseph, 60–61
Joubert, Lauren, 94

Kaminsky, Joel S., 66
Kant, Immanuel, 96
Keener, 18n13, 44n4
Kethe, William, 134
Kiergegaard, Søren, 79–82, 96–97, 127–28
Kipling, Rudyard, 126
Krosney, Herbert, 27
Kuschel, Karl-Josef, 4, 93n10, 105n4, 106

Lehman, David, 30
Lentulus, 26–27
Lewis, C. S., 131
Longenecker, 23–24
Lorenz, Konrad, 5
Ludovici, Anthony M., 92
Luther, Martin, 50, 69, 82–83

McAuley, James, 30–31
McClintock, John, 27
Malley, Ern, 30–31
Malley, Ethel, 31
Mary, Mother of Jesus, 17, 35
Mary, Mother of John, 45
Maximus the Confessor, 105
Moltmann, Jürgen, 104
Morreall, John, 11n4, 15, 72n2, 73, 90, 96, 97n15, 110, 121
Morton, Russell, 45
Moses, 35, 58
Murray, David, 75

Neri, Philip, 130
Niebuhr, Reinhold, 7, 21, 26, 81, 125, 127
Nietzsche, Friedrich, 26, 84
Nyssa, Gregory of, 104

Oeclampadius, 105

Palmer, Jerry, 12n7, 13n9
Palmer, Parker J., 128
Paul, the apostle, 74, 78, 86–87, 104, 106
Peter, the apostle, 45–46, 112, 124
Philagrios, 54
Philogelos, 54
Pilate, Pontius, 104
Plato, 14, 54, 76, 90–91
Price, Lucian, 26n6

Quintilian, 54

Rachel, 35–36
Radday, Yehuda Thomas, 26
Rahner, Hugo, 105n3
Rahner, Karl, 87, 126
Rebekah, 35–36, 66–67
Repplier, Agnes, 124
Rhoda, 45–46
Rice, Tim, 61
Roeckelein, Jon E., 12n6, 95

Sarah, 57, 62–65, 68, 74, 135
Sayers, Dorothy L., 22, 25, 80–81
Schleiermacher, Friedrich, 86n22
Schopenhauer, Arthur, 6, 96–97
Schwartz, Hans, 24n4
Sharpe, Robert, 15
Schneemelcher, Wilhelm, 2 n11
Screech, Michael A., 50n2, 122
Spencer, Herbert, 94–95
Spinoza, Baruch, 14
Stewart, Harold, 30
Strong, James, 27n9

Tennent, Timothy, xi
Theresa of Avila, 70
Thomas, Aquinas, 15, 83, 101
Torrance, T. F., 98–99
Trueblood, Elton, 26
Twain, Mark, 82

Vall, Gregory, 66
Vogel, Heinrich, 99
Voltaire, 133–34

150

NAME INDEX

Webber, Anthony Lloyd, 61
Whedbee, William, 58, 60–62, 110, 114
White, E. B., 7
Whitehead, A. N., 26

Zipporah, 35–36
Zwingli, Huldrych, 48

Scripture Index

Genesis

1–11	60
1:27	14, 86
6:6, 9	61
7:16	61
9:21	61
11:1	61
12–36	62
12:2	63
15:5	63
15:6	63
17:4	63
17:17	63, 74
18:10–12	74
21:6	57, 63, 135
21:9	64
21:18	65
26:6–11	67
26:34–5	67
28:6	67
31:8	67
35:29	67
37–50	61

1 Kings

18: 16–39	107
18:25–7	92

Nehemiah

8:12	85

Job

1–2	110–13
1:1–2:10	59
3–42	113–22
3:1–4:11	59
3:4	59

Psalms

2:2–5	92
2:4	10, 25, 43
8:4–6	116
37:12–5	76
37:13	16, 25, 43
59:8	16, 25
78:2	38
126	74
126:2	52

Proverbs

1:6	38
1:26	103
3:34	103
13:1	103
15:12	103
17:15	85
19:29	103
21:24	103

Ecclesiastes

3:4	135

SCRIPTURE INDEX

Isaiah

5:23	85
6:8	58
35:10	10
44:1–20	107
53:2	26
60:20	52

Jeremiah

10:15	103
31:12	35
31:13	52

Ezekiel

17:2	38
20:49	38

Hosea

1:13	58
12:10	38

Joel

3:18	35

Amos

9:13–4	35

Sirach

21.20	ix
21.23	ix

Matthew

5:1–10	122
5:1–12	37
5:12	38, 56
5:13	48
5:14	48
5:29–30	38
5:33	48
5:37	108
6:2	42
6:3	48
6:34	87
7:6	49
7:16	49
7:26	42
8:22	51
10:37	37
11:18	36
11:25	37
13: 3–8	24n4
13:3–13, 34	38
13:44	41
14:13–21	53
15:14	39
16:16	46
18:2	33
18:3	48
18:23–25	18
18:23–35	38
19:24	49
20:16	52
21:28–32	42
22:18–22	50
23:5–7	43
23:27	43
23:24	49
23:25	43
23:27	44
24:33	42
25:5–7	43

Mark

2:19	49
4:2, 11, 33	38
4:3–8, 13–20	24n4
6:30–44	53
8:35	52
10:25	49
12:1–12	40
12:13–17	50
12:38–40	43
15:16–25	104

SCRIPTURE INDEX

Luke

1:46–55	17
1:47	87
2:10	55
5:34	49
6:20–6	37
6:21	103, 122
6:21, 25	52
6:24–25	52
6:39	39
6:41	49
6:46–49	42
7:34	36
8:4–8, 11–15	24n4
8:10	38
8:16	42
9:10–17	53
10:25–8	50
10:25–37	39
11:11–13	43
11:33	43
11:44	44
11:45	44
12:16–21	39
13:1–4	119
14:8–11	42
14:15–24	22–24, 38
14:28–30	42
14:31	42
14:34–35	48
15:1–32	41
15:7	56
16:9	50
16:1–12	40
16:14–15	40
18:1–8	39
18:9–14	39
18:16	37
18:9–14	39
18:16	37
20:9–19	40
22:31–4	112
22:63	104
24:52–3	55

John

2:1–12	35
2:13–14	108
2:11	35
3:3	48
3:8	132
3:27–30	35
4:1–42	35
4:29	36
6:1–15	53
6:35	48
10:7, 11	48
14:26	87
15	100
15:1	48
15:1–8	87
15:15	87
17:15	108

Acts

2:1–41	46
5:40	122
8:3	122
12	45–6
12:7	45

Romans

8:29	87

1 Corinthians

1:25	85
2:1–4	104
8:1–13	78
12:12–27	87
15:28	10
15:50–5	104
15:55	107

2 Corinthians

1:4, 6, 9	122
4:4	14
6:4	122
7:8	122
11:28	122

Ephesians

1:10	56
4:20–24	14
4:22–24	87
5:4	73

Philippians

1:12	122
3:10	122
4:8	78

Colossians

1:9–10	87
1:15–20	14
1:24–29	122
3:3–4	87
3:10	14

Hebrews

1:3	14
12:14	130

James

3:8–10	14
3:10	19

2 Peter

1:3–4	87
1:4	3, 133

1 John

4:8	84, 100
4:18	ix

Revelation

7:17	52
19:6–9	36
21:1–5	10
21:3–4	109
21:4	52